A PASSAGE TO KENYA

A Historical Collage of a Unique Time and Place

JOHN LAWRENCE NAZARETH

A PASSAGE TO KENYA

A Historical Collage of a Unique Time and Place

JOHN LAWRENCE NAZARETH

Copyright © 2017
John Lawrence Nazareth
All rights reserved.

ISBN: 1542732107
ISBN 13: 9781542732109
Library of Congress Control Number: 2017901202
CreateSpace Independent Publishing Platform
North Charleston, South Carolina

Dedicated to my wife, Abbey

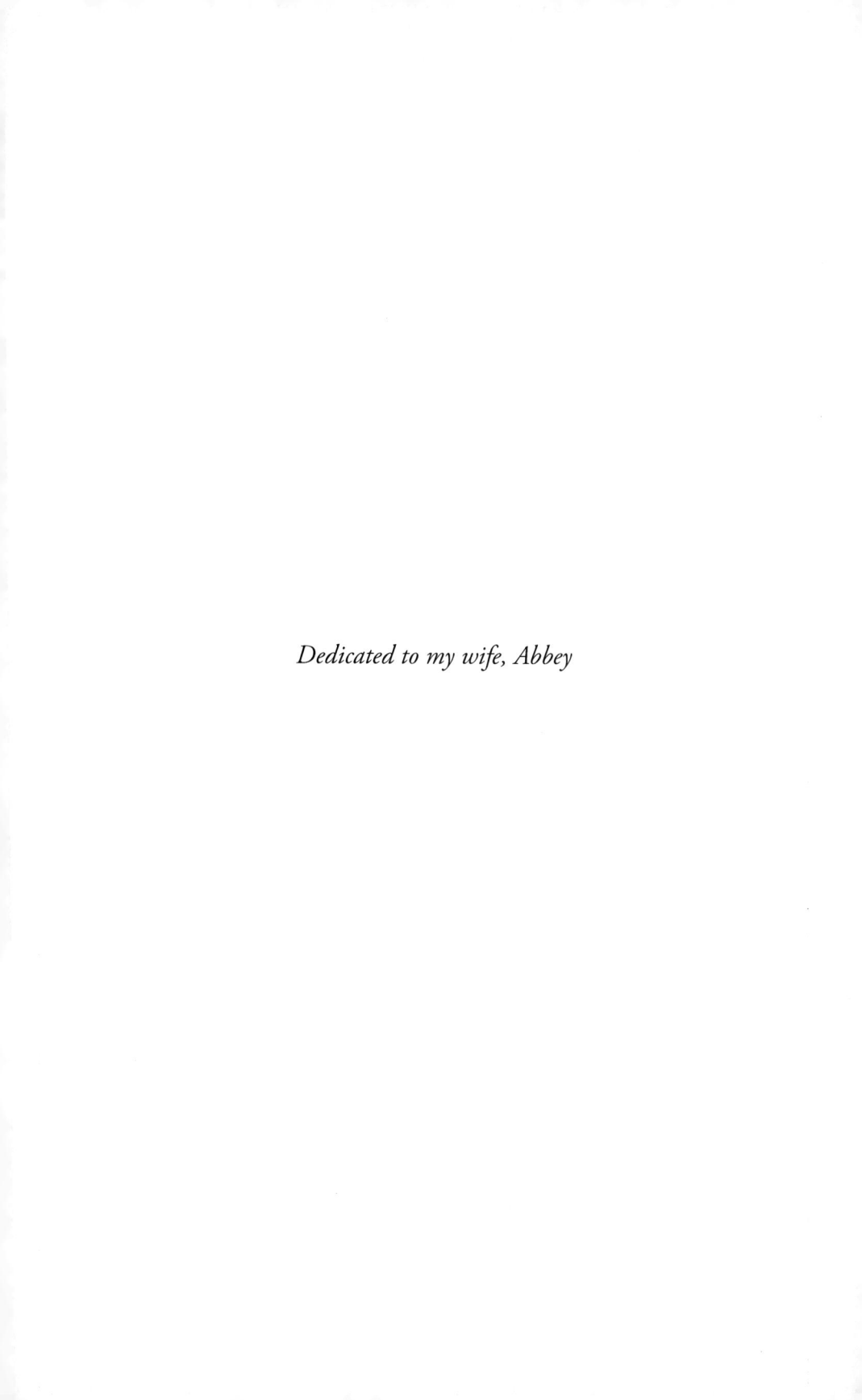

PREFACE

Every book has a particular genesis. But then it assumes a life of its own, which can take the writing in a direction quite different from the author's original intent. In the case of the present book, my initial impulse came from the desire to write a memoir of the years of my youth, of growing up within a complex mosaic of community, time, and place that embraced the then-British colony of Kenya where both my father and I were born, the newly-independent Republic of India that was formerly also under British rule, and the tiny Portuguese colony of Goa on India's west coast, which Portugal had refused to relinquish to independent India and from whence my paternal grandparents had emigrated to Kenya at the start of the 20th century. My intent was to weave in contextual information of a historical and familial nature, but, in the main, I wanted to write a personal "his-story" of life and circumstance in the two countries of my youth, Kenya and India.

In researching historical and familial background material for my planned memoir, I was fortunate to have access to an extensive library of books, many of them dealing with Kenya and India, which came into my hands following my father's death in 1989. They were shipped to me in the United States from Kenya, mailed in brown-paper packages tied up in string, each containing a dozen or so volumes, and they began to arrive on my doorstep at my home on an island in the Pacific North-West at regular intervals, over the course of several months during the early 1990s. At that time, being preoccupied with my own research and teaching within the mathematical sciences, I simply untied the packages, unwrapped the books, and put them away in newly-acquired bookcases. And there they remained, unread for well over a decade. But, when the time came to embark on writing the memoir outlined above, my father's library proved to be invaluable, a treasure-trove of useful background information on the two countries of my youthful years.

During the initial writing, I sought to mix both contextual and personal information. Repeatedly, I would stitch together and then unstitch sentences, paragraphs, entire chapters, but nothing seemed to work, even as the manuscript itself continued to grow significantly in length. The task became increasingly frustrating and I was ready to throw up my hands in despair and abandon the project when, of a sudden, it dawned on me that I was simultaneously at work on *two very different books*---that my frustration arose from trying to glue them together artificially into a single volume. Given that realization, everything fell much more easily into place. A portion of the by-then extensive manuscript, which had been the source of so much agonizing, gathered itself in a natural way into the first of the two books, which you now hold in your hands. And the remainder fell into a second, shorter book to be titled *Up and About in Nairobi and Bombay*---a collection of colorful vignettes that serves as a companion to the present book---which I hope to complete at a later date along the lines of my original conception. Much more reading, writing, and polishing remained to be done, but now all seemed to come more smoothly.

The present book is a journey through the colonial past of formerly-British Kenya and India and formerly-Portuguese Goa. More generally, it is a "biography" of the fascinating region that borders the Indian Ocean and an account of the extensive traffic and intercourse between the people of its diverse shores. The book has the character of a verbal *collage*, hence its subtitle "A Historical Collage of a Unique Time and Place." (Indeed the image used in the design of the cover highlights this particular feature of the book---I created it a few years ago when enrolled in an art course on beginner's collage at the Gage Institute in Seattle---and the hand-drawn maps and a handful of photographs within the text are employed likewise.) Throughout, I do not hesitate to quote directly and extensively from my source material, rather than summarizing such content in my own words, a style of writing inspired, for example, by William James---one of my heroes---in his classic *The Varieties of Religious Experience*. But, and here again following William James, *quotation is always in the service of a larger theme, or set of ideas, that one is seeking to convey*. I have used the device of highlighting particular sentences or phrases of a quotation by using italics, and by elaborating within a quotation when needed, by adding information in square brackets, for example, [clarifying material]. I have also sought to weave in my own personal views on the colonial experience within several of the chapters. In the writing, I was helped considerably by two books: the first, a memoir titled *Brown Man Black Country* published by my father, which describes his involvement in Kenyan politics and its march to independence from Britain in 1963, and the second, a travelogue detailing my extensive travels in India during the early 1980s, which I self-published under the title *Reminiscences of an Ex-Brahmin: Portraits of a Journey through India*. I have been able to utilize extracts from both these books in the present work.

Although this book is, most decidedly, not a biography of my father's life, a fortuitous outcome of its evolution, as described above, was that the life of my father---a brilliant lawyer and a principled, maverick politician---and also, but to a lesser extent, the story of my adventurous, paternal grandfather provided a *linking thread* that runs through the writing from beginning to end. And thus my book has turned out to be a special tribute to my father, as well as a thank you to both him and my mother, Maria Monica Freitas-Nazareth, for all the gifts, material and otherwise, that they bequeathed to me. Other immediate family members are mentioned here only in passing and I will honor them separately in the aforementioned, companion book of vignettes, *Up and About in Nairobi and Bombay*. As stated earlier, my primary purpose in this book is to present a historical collage of the colonial era and a personal commentary on the gross inequities of that exploitative, global economic-and-political system. Given the growing inequality of present-day globalization, I thus implicitly raise the question: are new, incorporated players, across trans-national boundaries, stepping into the roles of colonizer and colonized?

ACKNOWLEDGEMENTS:

I am especially grateful to my wife, Abbey, for her advice and valuable editorial assistance. Without her enthusiasm for my familial history and her encouragement that I tell it, this book would not have seen the light of day. I'm also very grateful to my brother, Lionel Nazareth, who, as described earlier, undertook the burdensome task of packaging and mailing to me the books from my deceased father's library, upon which my writing relies so heavily. And my thanks go again to him for his encouraging and helpful feedback and also to my sister, Jeanne Hromnik, for her insightful comments on my manuscript. Without explicitly naming names and thereby avoiding sins of omission, I thank my friends and relatives, both on and off island, for their interest and encouragement during this personal voyage of rediscovery of my historical past. And, last but not least, I thank the readers of this book and hope that they derive as much pleasure from perusing it as I did from its writing.

JLN
Bainbridge Island
Washington, USA
January, 2017

TABLE OF CONTENTS

Preface vii

Chapter 1   Origins 1
Chapter 2   Explorers and Exploiters 14
Chapter 3   The Lunatic Line 29
Chapter 4   My Pioneering Grandfather 41
Chapter 5   Golden Goa Turned to Clay 56
Chapter 6   Church, Caste, and Club 80
Chapter 7   Mackie Will Make My Name 96
Chapter 8   Kenyan Pioneers 103
Chapter 9   On Indian Independence 129
Chapter 10 First Steps 137
Chapter 11 The Mau Mau Eruption 155
Chapter 12 J.M. Nazareth, Q.C., M.L.C. 197

Bibliography 209
Author's Biography 215

Chapter 1

ORIGINS

My father, John Cazimir Maximian Nazareth, demonstrated his hallmark independence of mind at a very early age when he discarded his middle name, 'Cazimir', which he had apparently found to be distasteful. He thus chose to go officially as J.M. Nazareth, but to family and friends he was known as Max, or, more affectionately, Mackie. He was born near the end of the first decade of the twentieth century, in the newly-colonized land of Kenya, a British Protectorate---perhaps, more accurately, a British *Exploitorate*---that straddled the equator below the horn of eastern Africa. Today, more than a century later, Kenya is an independent nation of forty million inhabitants and in the limelight as it has never been before, primarily because the twice-elected president of the United States, Barack Obama, traces his ancestral roots to that distant part of the world. But, at the time of my father's birth, Kenya was virgin territory for colonial Britain. Its present-day capital, the city of Nairobi, located on the mile-high plains of central Kenya, about 300 miles from the coast, was then little more than a rest stop on a railway line that the British---again, more accurately, Great Britain's brown and black colonial subjects---were building, from the port of Mombasa to the inland territory of Uganda, at the headwaters of the river Nile.

The year was 1899 and one of these brown subjects was an enterprising man of impressive girth and imposing beard, my paternal grandfather Joachim Antonio Nazareth. At least that is how I pictured him, because I knew my grandfather only from a framed photograph that hung, larger than life, on a living room wall in the house of my Aunty Nathu---his eldest daughter Natividad. Sadly, my grandfather had passed away more than a decade and a half before my own birth in 1946, and he was buried in the Catholic cemetery near the foot of Forest Road, a half-mile down from the house where we lived in Nairobi. I'd bicycle daily past the low-lying stone wall that bordered this cemetery, on my way to school, youthfully oblivious of my grandfather's adventurous and colorful past. And little did I know at that time that my father, following instructions given shortly before he passed away in 1989, would also be laid to rest within the grave of his father, Joachim Antonio; and that almost twenty years later, some of my mother's ashes would be scattered at that same gravesite, in a cemetery by then long abandoned and grown wild.

When my grandfather first arrived in Kenya, he was very likely beardless and much less prosperous-looking than the man in the photograph on Aunty Nathu's wall. He came as one of the anonymous workers from India who provided the muscle and brain for the British expansion into eastern Africa, but were nevertheless denigrated by the rulers of the British empire as "Indian coolies." Family lore has it that he arrived by dhow at the port of Mombasa, at a time when the railway line being built from the coast to the shores of Lake Victoria in Uganda was only half-way complete. And thus began an adventure where his fortunes rose and then declined precipitously, as we will relate in a subsequent chapter.

India at the time of my grandfather's migration was a colony of Great Britain, its so-called "jewel in the crown." There was no partition between India and Pakistan and Bangladesh. The British ruled the entire region, a subcontinent shaped rather like a duck's bottom, which stretched from the broad Himalayan range in the north to its southern, pointed tip near the island of Ceylon, present-day Sri Lanka. Beginning with a small trading post on the site of Madras (today's Chennai), which was granted by the Hindu rulers of the south in 1639, the British had extended their control by degrees, eventually triumphing in a four-way struggle for control of the Indian subcontinent. The other three protagonists in this struggle were the Indianized-Muslim rulers of the north, whose series of incursions, beginning in the twelfth century A.D., had culminated in control over a large part of India during the reign of the great emperor Akbar (1555-1606); the Maharatas of western India who were finally crushed by the British in 1818; and the French, in alliance with the Hindu Kings of southern India, whose fortunes in India were intimately linked with those of Napoleon in Europe, and whose last vestiges of influence are now apparent only in places like Pondicherry (south of Madras, today's Chennai). The memorable year 1776, when the North Americans finally shook themselves free of the British, is also the year when the people of India had begun to almost completely lose their freedom *to* the British, establishing hegemony over the subcontinent that lasted for approximately one hundred and fifty years. The British unified this diverse land by building an extensive network of railways and introducing spoken and written English to a people compartmentalized by dozens of languages, hundreds of dialects, and a half-dozen different scripts. Delhi, both New and Old, Karachi, Bombay, Madras, Calcutta were the colony's principal cities, and it was at the port of Karachi that my grandfather embarked on his voyage to the Kenyan Protectorate. However, his journey was via rather than originating from Karachi, because my grandfather was not a resident and subject of British India at that time. His place of origin was Portuguese Goa on India's west coast, approximately a third of the way from Bombay

3

to the southern tip. This little dimple of a colony was a relic of a much earlier time when Portugal was the dominant power over the trading routes of the Indian Ocean and had established Goa as its eastern headquarters. We will have much more to relate later about Goa's golden age during the 16th and 17th centuries and its subsequent long decline, but suffice it now to say that when my grandparents decided to emigrate at the end of the 19th century, Goa was a slumbering, backwater colony, a tiny remaining fragment of Portugal's long-lost empire, which Britain had felt no apparent need to appropriate. Like the Portugal of that time, Goa was haunted by the echoes and ghosts of its earlier golden era and it offered little hope of advancement to men of ambition like my grandfather. The colony's principal towns, Panjim and Marmagoa, near the colony's two excellent harbors, served as its administrative centers, but the bulk of Goa's inhabitants lived in villages, whose number exceeded three hundred, and labored within an agriculture-based economy. The Goa that my grandfather chose to leave was a Goa at its nadir.

What of East Africa on the other side of the Indian Ocean to which he immigrated to make a new home? Its coast, extending from the horn of Africa to the continent's southern cape, has an extraordinarily rich and variegated past. Ships and sailors from ancient Phoenicia, the Roman Empire, even far-distant Imperial China, have touched its shores, and over the course of many centuries, the coastal region has seen extensive cultural overlap and genetic intermingling of peoples of diverse origin---African, Arab, Persian, Indian, even Indonesian. But, until the mid-1800s, the East African *interior* had remained mysterious, penetrated by outsiders only along a few well-travelled "caravan" routes. This region belonged, over the millennia, to a multitude of African tribes, living within a continent that contains many hidden secrets about the lineage of the human species. Its dominant geographic feature, the Great Rift Valley, which extends in a fractured pattern southward for two thousand miles from the Red Sea to Mozambique, is like a giant taproot that has nourished the spread of both ancient and modern strains of humanity, from the African continent to the far reaches of the globe. This is where the famous self-taught paleontologist, Louis Leakey, made his great discoveries of our distant ancestors, notably at Olduvai Gorge in today's Tanzania, and where further north in Ethiopia was found one of the most famous skeletons of ancient woman, the diminutive Lucy. Southern and eastern Africa today is thought to be the crucible of interchanging forestland and savannah where modern man and woman---Homo Sapiens and Homa Sapiens, so to speak--first evolved, approximately 200,000 years ago. By studying human populations and their genetic markers, migration routes have been traced, which began some 50,000-60,000 years ago, out of Africa to all the other continents; and one of the most ancient is conjectured to be from the horn of Africa, across the coastal areas of the Arabian peninsula and the mid-East, southward along the Indian subcontinent, and then across the Indonesian archipelago to northern Australia. The climate was much cooler and ocean levels were much lower at that time, and thus vast areas of the continental shelf were exposed, providing relatively easy travel routes along the shoreline, with a rich supply of food. New Guinea and Australia, in particular, were very likely bulbous parts of a single continent, joined by a narrow isthmus now reclaimed by the sea. Along this route, the aboriginal people of Australia first reached their homeland, whose northern reaches lie, coincidentally, at roughly the same latitude as southern East Africa, where they became isolated by the rising waters of the ocean. I imagine their hunter-gatherer way of life as being akin to that of the Bushmen and Hottentots of South-West Africa and the East African tribe known as the Wanderobo, relatively unchanged for tens of thousands of years, and representative of the very *root-stock* of humanity. This Africa-to-Australia migration route is now known to be only one of many, as humanity spread out across all the continents and rebounded back again into Africa, a history preserved today within the continent's magnificent and unmatched diversity of tribe and language.

Historical and archeological evidence suggest that well over two thousand years ago, perhaps even much further back dating to a time that predates the Aryan conquest, the Dravidians of South India---the original inhabitants of the subcontinent before it was invaded by Aryan tribes from the north---had extensive knowledge of eastern and southern Africa. They had come primarily to explore and prospect for gold, bringing with them the coconut palm, the mango, and many other non-indigenous flora. Later the great Buddhist Emperor Ashoka (3rd Century, B.C.), whose empire encompassed much of the Indian subcontinent, is known to have maintained a large fleet, as did his Hindu Gupta successors during the period called the Golden Age of India. And almost any history of Africa will mention the *Periplus of the Erythrean Sea*, circa 80 A.D., an ancient Romano-Greek navigational manual, which documents Indian and Arab ships trading along the East African coast. All this ancient contact is now shrouded in mystery. For example, Negley Farson's 1940 travelogue *Behind God's Back,* describing travels in East Africa, contains the following curious passage:

> "...then [I saw] the blue distances of the Great Rift, with its bronze volcanoes! That day I had driven around a volcano into which the groove of an old Phoenician trail disappeared---and began again on the other side. Which proved, said my hostess, that the volcano had erupted since the Phoenicians had worn that trail in search of gold."

But, if one substitutes "Dravidian" for "Phoenician" and recalls the 1930 discovery, or should one say rediscovery, of a rich gold vein near a town called Kakamega in north-western Kenya, the foregoing conjecture regarding ancient penetration of the interior suddenly becomes quite credible. Indeed, the African continent is apparently mentioned in the ancient Holy Books of the Hindus and it is said that when the nineteenth century English explorer John Speke, who had once served in the military in British India, rediscovered the source of the river Nile, he was able to make use of these old Indian descriptions.

The Chinese also had extensive contact with the lands around the Indian Ocean. As far back as the Tang Dynasty in the 8th century A.D., Chinese vessels regularly called at Sofala, located on the African mainland opposite the island of Madagascar. Trade in the region was dominated at that time by Arabian ships, centering on ivory, ambergris, and gold from inland mines (along with the centuries-old traffic in slaves to the Arabian Peninsula), in which pursuit the Chinese may perhaps have sought to cut out the Arab middleman. Chinese voyages of trade and discovery continued intermittently and reached their peak during the Ming Dynasty in the early fifteenth century. Fleets of magnificent junks, primarily three-masters, but occasionally with as many as six masts and a crew of six hundred sailors, traversed the Indian Ocean and the Arabian Sea. During one of those voyages, sometime within the period 1417-1419, it is reported that a large fleet, under the command of a renowned Chinese Admiral named Cheng Ho, touched briefly at the port of Malindi, just north of Mombasa on the East African coast, a locale made famous almost a century later by the arrival of the first Portuguese explorer, Vasco da Gama. And, of course, one should not fail to mention the famed Venetian traveler to the Far East, Marco Polo, who was able to draw on knowledge gained from China to write of Indian ships "which visit the island of Madeigascar and the other of Zanghibar," present day Madagascar and Zanzibar, in a travelogue that helped to inspire the voyages of discovery of Christopher Columbus and his successors. In an astonishing turn of events, the Chinese Emperor by edict banned further voyages of exploration in the year 1433, and China withdrew into itself, just when Europe was beginning to reach outward, first into the South Atlantic, then across the North Atlantic in search of a route to India, and eventually around southern Africa to the Indian Ocean.

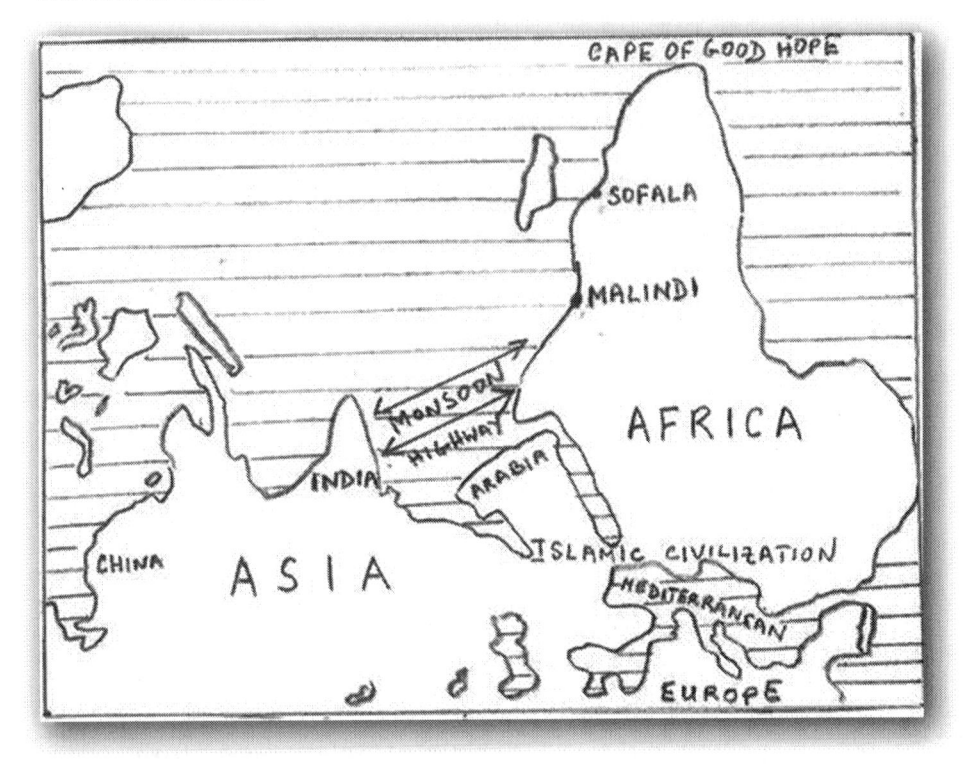

The world looked very different to Europeans of that time. A little trick, which the historian and adventurer, Michael Wood, has famously used to capture the ancient Greek view of the world, can equally capture this pre-Columbian perspective. As the foregoing figure depicts, Wood *inverts* a modern map of Europe, Asia, and Africa---the Americas and Australia were unknown to Europeans before 1492---so that our modern "south" becomes the inverted map's "north," our direction "down" instead becomes "up". This device also serves to bring into the foreground the so-called negative space---an artist's term for the map's shaded area---and this completely alters one's visualization of the globe. India is seen to lie at the very *center* of this "old" world, in keeping with its stature at that time, linked to Arabia and eastern Africa by the age-old "monsoon highway," whose winds blow across the Indian Ocean toward Africa from November to March and in the opposite direction from May to September. This highway made possible the extensive sailing-traffic between Asia and Africa. The Red Sea and a short overland trip (across where Africa is connected to Asia) also provided a trading route to the lands surrounding the Mediterranean Sea. A resplendent Islamic civilization stretched across this region, to the "north" of the Mediterranean and across central Asia, keeping alive the heritage of Greece and transmitting the advances of Indian science, mathematics, and medicine to a Europe newly awakened during the fifteenth century.

This was the period of the early Renaissance, when Leonardo da Vinci, Michelangelo, Copernicus and others, initiated a great revolution in the arts and sciences. It is worth remembering that in 1492, the year that Columbus landed in the Americas, these three great geniuses had yet to create the masterpieces for which they are best known---the Mona Lisa, the Sistine Chapel, and the heliocentric, or sun-centered, theory of the planets; King Henry the Eighth had yet to ascend the English throne and separate the Church of England from Roman Catholicism; and the flowering marked by the reigns of three of the world's greatest monarchs---Henry's daughter Elizabeth I of England, Philip II of Spain, and the Indian-Mogul Emperor Akbar whose grandson later built the Taj Mahal---lay well into the future. The *reawakening* of Europe, which coincided with the voyages of discovery of European mariners of the fifteenth century, served to *reinvert* the map of Michael Wood's invention, of which we have just spoken. It placed Europe at the "top" of the world, where it remains to the present day.

Sent forth by the renowned Prince Henry-the-Navigator, Portuguese mariners circumnavigated for the first time the tip of southern Africa---the Cape of Good Hope---and reached the coast of East Africa. These explorations were undertaken in a very systematic way, beginning early in the fifteenth century when the Chinese were withdrawing into a self-imposed isolation. The great pioneer of this southern route was Bartholomew Diaz, followed by an explorer of even greater renown, Vasco da Gama, who landed in 1498 north of Mombasa at Malindi, the very port visited by a Chinese fleet at the beginning of the same century. His ships were then piloted across the Indian Ocean by an Indian sailor whose true identity is lost to history. Some say he originated from the Malabar Coast, others assert that he was a Hindu named Cana or Kahna (variants on the name of the Hindu god Krishna), and yet others, more plausibly, that his name was Ahmad ibn Majid from the Muslim-dominated state of Gujerat. Today, not far from the site where Vasco da Gama landed in East Africa, one can still find the remains of an ancient Hindu phallic temple, itself located beside a mosque of more recent origin. And on display in the museum of the nearby ruins of Gedi, a thriving Arab settlement during the 12th–16th centuries A.D., are fragments of Ming Dynasty pottery and ancient Chinese coins. The coastal area of eastern Africa is littered with mysteries such as these, as are places further inland where African tribesmen exhibit genetic and linguistic traces of an intercourse, in the far distant past, with the peoples of ancient India.

The Portuguese soon put an end to the Arab domination of the coast and began to leave their own enduring relics on the land, the most imposing being Fort Jesus in Mombasa, built in 1591, which stands to this day. But the coast of East Africa served primarily as a point of transit to India where the Portuguese established the flourishing sixteenth-century city at Goa on India's west coast, a center for their maritime trade, of which we shall have much to relate in a subsequent chapter. To safeguard this route, the Portuguese built a "rosary" of forts, in particular, near Aden on the Arabian Peninsula and at Muscat, near the Straits of Hormuz, thereby effectively cutting off both the Red Sea and the

Persian Gulf to Arab traders, and forcing trade along the southern route that they controlled. The Portuguese grip on the trade routes and their period of ascendancy across the Indian Ocean lasted for two centuries, but was eventually broken by the Dutch, who were also in search of territory and profit in Africa and South-East Asia. (Recall that the Boers of South Africa were Dutch in origin, and that the Dutch were the dominant power over Indonesia from the seventeenth to the mid-twentieth century.) The Arabs of Oman were then able to return during the 1700s to a renewed control over the eastern coast of Africa.

It was during the reign of Sultan Seyyid Said of Oman, commencing in the first decade of the nineteenth century, that the sleepy island of Zanzibar, near the coastline of East Africa, began to flourish and assume a unique character, which survives to the present day. In 1832, Sultan Said did something quite remarkable: he moved his capital from Muscat in Oman to the island of Zanzibar and began to rule his kingdom on the southern Arabian Peninsula from the East African coast, rather than the other way around. He introduced clove plantations to the island and to the neighboring island of Pemba, which were soon yielding *four-fifths* of the world's production of this spice. Many of the tall white houses, built from coral limestone along Zanzibar's harbor, date back to this period. Soon Zanzibar became a trading port known across the globe. In addition to cloves, exports included ivory brought from the interior, raw materials, for example, copra, hides, and rubber, and of course, sadly, slaves captured on the mainland. The most important import was cotton cloth (called "Amerakani" in the local language of Swahili because much of it came from the United States), and necessities like rice, guns, and hardware. Interestingly enough, it was the United States among the western powers that was the first to establish a consulate in Zanzibar in 1836---well before the American Civil War that ended slavery in North America---and soon was followed by the British consulate in 1841. The British were the dominant power across the Indian Ocean at this time, ruling India, South Africa, Mauritius, and other smaller islands, but they were only just beginning to take an interest in eastern Africa.

During Said's reign, Zanzibar became, in the words of the world-traveler John Gunter, "the biggest and most hideous slave *entrepot* in the world." Slaves captured in the East African interior were brought to Zanzibar by caravans that were financed by merchants based in the island, and from there these unfortunates were bought by other intermediaries and shipped to near and distant places: the sugar plantations on the islands of Mauritius and Reunion in the Indian Ocean; Southern Arabia, Persia, and north-west to India; and a few were even shipped around the Cape of Good Hope to Spanish and Portuguese plantations in South America. It is not inconceivable that some slaves from East Africa were even taken to the southern United States.

The phasing out of slavery in East Africa began with the arrival of the British. The new mode of production based on industrialization, along with the newly-awakened forces of conscience, were putting an end to slavery. An Act of Parliament passed in 1807 had made it illegal for a British person or British ship to participate in the slave trade. But, as they were often wont to do---let us not forget that, in previous centuries, Great Britain had been a leading participant in the slave trade from western Africa to its colonies in North America and the Caribbean and had profited greatly from it---the British reached a compromise with the Sultan of Zanzibar. In 1822, this agreement outlawed the transshipment of slaves eastwards to India or south of a line across the Indian Ocean that corresponded roughly with the southern border of modern-day Tanzania. But it did not prevent shipment of slaves to the Arabian Peninsula. The slaves who were kept in Zanzibar or elsewhere on the East Africa coast, to work on local clove plantations or in other forms of servitude, were the luckier ones. Their suffering was great, but undoubtedly the ones transported overseas suffered more horribly. The British eventually outlawed slavery altogether and freed existing slaves, and the completion of the Ugandan railway at the start of the twentieth century, which rendered the old slave caravan routes obsolete, was its final death knell. One of the earliest colonial officials and administrators of the new order being imposed by the British was the scholarly Charles W. Hobley, who makes the following curious summary of this closing chapter in the history of East African slavery (see his *Kenya: From Chartered Company to Crown Colony*):

> "I was, myself, for years in close touch with thousands of domestic slaves on the East Coast of Africa, and can testify that their bondage was very light, the treatment of the slaves was extraordinarily humane, and they were a contented people. The Arab is naturally a lazy person, and rarely had the energy to work his slaves as a European owner would do. .....
>
> I look upon the enslaving of human beings with abhorrence, but the disruption of a social organization, such as domestic slavery, has to be carried out with the greatest caution, or ruin results. The procedure actually adopted on the coast of what is now called Kenya Protectorate ruined both masters and slaves.
>
> The Arab even now, in his heart, fails to understand why we are so uncompromising about slavery; it is recognized by the Koran, as that is good enough for him. That he is hopelessly impoverished by its abolition is admitted by all, for the compensation awarded to him was small, and it was soon squandered; he was never able to adjust himself to the new order of things, his extensive cultivated lands soon reverted to jungle, and remain jungle today."

Ownership and control of the East African coast was changing hands from Arab to British and German. *All was once again in flux!*

Chapter 2

EXPLORERS AND EXPLOITERS

Arab slave traders had penetrated far inland, but their journeys of evil were confined in the main to just a few well-travelled caravan routes. It was only during the great era of European exploration that began in the mid-nineteenth century that the geography and ethnography of East Africa became revealed to the outside world. The men (and a few women) who ventured into the interior, British and German in the main, were either missionaries of various denominations, who came to save souls, or adventurers of a much rougher hue. Many of their names are now legendary. In 1848-49, the German missionaries Ludwig Krapf and J. Rebmann reported the *discovery* of snow-capped mountains at the equator to an incredulous Europe. (One should, of course, hasten to add that the native Kikuyu and Chagga tribesmen, who lived at that time in the foothills of these mountains, were hardly *uninformed* about their existence.) During the period 1857-62, the English explorers John Speke, James Grant, and Richard Burton, under the sponsorship of the Royal Geographical Society, identified the source of the Nile as being a great inland lake, subsequently named for Queen Victoria, and the source of the River Congo as being the long, narrow and very deep Lake Tanganyika. Soon afterwards, Speke met up with Samuel Baker, another extraordinary character, who had journeyed southward along the Nile, also in search of its source, traversing the Sud in Southern Sudan, which Piers Brendon, in his monumental tome *The Decline and Fall of the British Empire,* describes as

> "... the world's most stupendous morass, a product of the Nile's transcontinental incontinence. Clogged with reeds, papyrus and rotting vegetation, it was a Sargasso Sea in the desert. Alive with crocodiles, hippopotamuses and mosquitoes, it was a slimy, noxious spawning ground of pestilence and death. Baker and his beautiful, blond Hungarian wife endured sickness, encountered cannibals and fought against mutiny and desertion among his porters."

Baker's disappointment at not being the first to identify the source of the Nile was great, but his consolation prize was to "discover" a smaller, intermediary lake, located subserviently downstream from Lake Victoria, and thus, perhaps very appropriately, to name it Lake Albert, after Queen Victoria's husband.

Piers Brendon provides vivid and colorful description of these ferocious characters: "Burton reminded people of a caged black leopard. He had a muscular frame, a barrel chest,"---and here quoting another writer---"a countenance the most sinister I have ever seen, dark, cruel, treacherous, with eyes like a wild beast's." Apparently "Burton liked to boast that he had indulged in every vice and committed every crime." At an earlier date, in India, "Burton rode alligators, charmed snakes, and became the army's most brilliant linguist. He eventually mastered more than two dozen languages and many dialects, even trying to learn simian speech from a troupe of monkeys he installed in his house." Brendon, likewise, describes Samuel Baker as "a great bear of a man, with a gruff, bluff manner and a shaggy black beard; he was primarily a hunter and an adventurer. No one was more dedicated to the massacre of game (unless it was John Hanning Speke, discoverer of Lake Victoria, who liked to eat the fetuses of pregnant animals he killed)." Baker liked to "live off boiled hippo head (which when served with chopped onions, salt and cayenne pepper 'throws brawn completely in the shade')." As for the explorer Stanley, Brendon notes that "even Burton disapproved of the tyrannical methods employed in Africa by Henry Morton Stanley. He 'shoots negroes as if they were monkeys,' Burton complained. However, Stanley's most recent biographer disputes this, pointing out his hero was less racist than Burton and less bloodstained than Baker." These dubious virtues notwithstanding, Stanley's main claim to fame relies on his legendary rendez-vous with the Scottish missionary David Livingstone, who played a pivotal role in the movement to eliminate slavery in East Africa. Their "Dr. Livingstone, I presume" encounter in 1871 at Ujiji, the little port on the inland Lake Tanganyika at the terminus of an ancient caravan route, is known to all.

Missionaries and explorers had approached Lake Victoria from the south, using well-traveled slave caravan routes that skirted the Masai territory, where they were safer from attack. Consequently, the more direct route from Mombasa to the lake, in a north-westerly direction, remained unexplored for almost another twenty years. It was not until 1882 that Joseph Thomson, under commission from the Royal Geographic Society, led a memorable expedition that traversed this northern route, encountering a veritable symphony of musically-named African landmarks along the way: the *Ngong* Hills, the lands of the *Kikuyu*, down the Rift Valley and past the extinct volcano called *Longonot* and the inland lake *Naivasha*, across the Aberdare mountains (named for the then-President of the Royal Geographic Society) and the foothills of Mt. Kenya to the region known as the *Kavirondo*, and finally past another inland body of water called *Baringo* to the northern-eastern shores of Lake Victoria, the ancients' *Ukerewe* Sea.

Lest one think that these intrepid spirits simply landed at the coast and immediately proceeded inland on their adventurous explorations, it is worth remembering that there was a considerable "infrastructure" in place to organize and outfit a caravan for the journey---a *safari* in the native Swahili language. (For example, as Charles Hobley points out, the word "safari" comes from the Arabic "safir," which means "the going" and it is generally translated as "caravan.") Zanzibar was the location where one recruited natives willing to go into the interior, and all caravans originated there until the Imperial British East Africa Company, in the late nineteenth century, made it possible for Mombasa to also provide a staging ground. There was a long established tradition of the slave and ivory transporting caravans being led by Arabs and financed---not to their credit---by Indians. Hobley gives a good description of the formalized procedure for organizing such a caravan, as does that old scoundrel, John Boyes, in a memoir *King of the Wa-Kikuyu,* which can be quoted verbatim:

> "Porters were chiefly Swahili, a name meaning 'coast dwellers.' These Swahili considered themselves more civilized than the people of the interior. They practice the Mohammedan religion and copy the Arabs in their dress. Swahili porters march under a headman of their own race, who receives his orders and repeats them to his followers. If, as sometimes happens, there are porters from other native tribes in the caravan, each tribe has its representative headman. For each ten carriers there is an *askari*, or soldier, who is armed with a rifle, and whose duty is to keep guard at night and protect the caravan on the road. The askaris also act as police and keep order generally, and bring in any deserters. As may be easily imagined, it would hardly do to trust merely in the askaris' sense of duty for the prevention of desertion, but

a clearly understood condition of their engagement in that capacity ensures their using their best endeavours to prevent anything of the sort. It is the recognized rule on all *safaris* that, if any man of the ten in an askari's section deserts, and the askari cannot bring him back, he will himself have to carry the deserters load for the rest of the journey. Apart from the unpleasantness of having to carry a sixty-pound load in the ranks of the porters instead of swaggering along with no other burden than his rifle, ammunition, and blanket, the blow to his self-importance involved in the degradation from askari to porter is one that would be severely felt ... ."

The general procedure was to try and hire a capable principal headman, who would then select a set of junior headmen, and each of the latter then collected his squad of porters, subject to approval from above. The usual equation was one headman for fifty porters and, as just mentioned, one askari for ten porters, the former being promoted from the porters' ranks and subject to demotion. Within this overall pattern, it was not uncommon to outfit caravans with five or six hundred men---sometimes as many as a thousand---and, as Hobley points out, "this entailed organization of a high character, and great skill in handling the natives."

It was by these means that the early European explorers were able to traverse the land and obtain a good overall picture of its topography and the peoples that inhabited it. You will see a brief summary in the two maps at the end of this chapter. You see the long-inhabited coral islands of Zanzibar and Pemba; the three main rivers, Tana, Athi, and Pangani, which could be raging torrents in the wet season and shrink to a trickle in the dry; the two main mountains, Kenya and Kilimanjaro; and the overall fractures of the eastern and western branches of the Great Rift Valley with their lakes and volcanoes, the eastern rift having very marked walls in the region between the two great mountains that lie to its east, but petering out further south, and the western running in a semi-circle that contains long, narrow lakes, in particular, Lake Tanganyika. You see Lake Victoria, the largest of the inland lakes and the source of the Nile River, which lies in between the two branches of the Rift Valley. And you see the overall three-fold pattern of narrow coastal plain, a central plateau where much of the territory is either dry grassland or arid desert, and highland areas and lands bordering on them, where the relatively small proportion of land best suited to cultivation is to be found.

And, on the second map of the tribal people of East Africa, you see the early slaving caravan routes, indicated by solid lines originating from the early coastal settlements---Pangani, Bagamoyo, and Kilwa---and forever marked by the bones of thousands who perished along them. And you see the names and locales of some of the larger or more prominent tribes: the Nilo-Hamitic Masai; the Bantu Kikuyu, Kamba, Chagaa, Kavirondo and Baganda; and the Nilotic Luo, a list that omits numerous other, much smaller tribes of Eastern Africa, a few of which are named on the map. In the vast central grassy areas, the nomadic Masai were dominant, roaming freely to steal cattle and women, their raiding parties often penetrating all the way to the coast. In the forested highlands, the Kikuyu were settled in agricultural villages on the eastern side of the Rift extending up to the foothills of Mount Kenya, and the Kavirondo peoples on the western side. To the south, the Chagaa peoples cultivated the richer foothill areas of Kilimanjaro. And around the shores of Lake Victoria, the Baganda held sway within a feudal system that was perhaps the most developed region of East Africa. The area around Lake Victoria, which was traditionally called the Ukerewe Sea prior to European exploration and so-named on the second map, was especially rich in productive potential. For example, John Speke, in his fascinating *Journal of the Discovery of the Source of the Nile,* describes the southern approach to the lake in his journey from the ancient caravan center of Kazeh (today's Tabora) as being rich and picturesque:

"The country here, so different from the Ujiji line, affords not only delightful food for the eyes, but abounds in flesh, milk, eggs, and vegetables and in every variety. ……

The whole country lies in long waves, contrasted with cropping little hills, thickly clad with small trees and brushwood. In the hollows of these waves the cultivation is very luxuriant. …."

He mentions, in particular, the cultivation of coffee and cotton, observes large herds of cattle, and notes that there were hardly any trees of any girth and that the land contained significant mineral wealth:

"The sandstone is highly impregnated with iron, and smelters do a good business. Indeed all the iron for nearly all the tools and cutlery that are used in this division of East Africa is found and manufactured here."

Lest you assume that elsewhere the tribal peoples of East Africa and other parts of the continent led isolated existences, it is worth commenting further on their means of communication and their mode of commerce and transportation, primitive by the technological standards of the time, but nevertheless adequate for their needs. John Boyes in his aforementioned memoir notes the following communication methods:

"The Kikuyu shouts his news from hill to hill, while the Masai runner thinks no more of carrying a message sixty miles in a day than we would of a three-mile stroll; the Congolese have a system of whistle signals, by which they can convey messages from one end of a district to the other in a very short time; while the West African native tells his news from village to village by means of a sort of Morse code [actually it is more akin to a form of shorthand], tapped out on drums. The Matabele [a tribe of Southern Africa] uses a system of signaling by long and short obscurations of a fire by means of a skin, or in the daytime by long and short puffs of smoke regulated by the same means ……. By these various means it is quite possible to convey news over enormous distances in a remarkably short space of time …"

Primitive currencies were also in use for commerce across East Africa. These consisted of a variety of commodities knows as "trade goods" and they provided the medium for exchange. They were part of the sixty-pound load carried by each porter on the journey inland and were used by the leaders of the caravan expedition to buy favor, ensure safe passage, purchase food, etc. Typical goods consisted of a variety of cloths traded in prescribed measurements, e.g., the length of a forearm, for which there were well-established relative values; beads in a variety of shapes (round, oval, rings) and colors (pink, white, dark blue, rich red), each with identifiable Swahili names and relative values, and traded in bundles of about a pound each; brass and iron wire of a prescribed thickness and diameter; and even cowrie shells, threaded in strings of one hundred. A particularly interesting unit of currency around the eastern area of Lake Victoria was the hoe made of iron, which was smelted locally by tribes in the Kavirondo area. And, of course, there were the ubiquitous cattle and sheep. As an example of exchange values, two or three hoes were the equivalent of a sheep, and thirty hoes the equivalent of a cow; one hoe was the equivalent of fifteen strings of pink pound beads, and so on. For the reader interested in such matters, additional, delightful detail can be found in an appendix of Charles Hobley's aforementioned memoir.

As for transportation, the noticeable absence of use of the wheel has been said to evidence the backward nature of the tribal people of East Africa. But these are people who, as we have just seen, were perfectly capable of the much more difficult task of smelting and shaping iron.

In contrast, note that a primitive wooden cart-wheel is an exceedingly simple device. I once saw an example used by early pioneers on the North American continent, comprising a solid circular wooden disk with a hole drilled at the center. A short cylindrical shaft extended from the main body of a cart to fit the hole, and on which the wheel could roll, this shaft being pegged on the outside to prevent the wheel from slipping off. That was the extent of it!

There are, in fact, a host of reasons that explain why the wheel was not suited to the East African countryside. Carts need roads, and roads were not easy to build given the nature of the soil and the torrential rains that easily washed them away. Draft animals are needed to draw the carts, and animals that were available in East Africa, for example, zebras or wildebeests, were not easily domesticated and would have been subject to attack by the predators that normally preyed on them in the wild. Imported draft animals like camels and horses died quickly and would have also been subject to similar attack. Bullocks were difficult to use because of lack of water and infection from disease-carrying tsetse flies that infested a large part of the country. And, of course, one needs a form of commerce within the region that, in turn, calls for animal-drawn carts. It is necessary only to read the works of Jared Diamond to understand the deeper, geographical-based reasons for why the wheel was not adopted and why human transport by caravan, sadly often provided by slaves, was the most suitable way of moving goods across the East African countryside. We will see this again in the next chapter when we come to the construction of a more modern form of caravan, the one that travels on rails.

Europeans with their far-superior technology had little difficulty gaining the upper hand over the tribal people of East Africa, and it is useful to conclude with Hobley's description of the growth of political control by the British administrative power, which is highly revealing of the European mindset of the time. Although not stated explicitly, the ruthlessness and the savagery of the process will be readily apparent. I have yet to encounter anything more instructive on how the British gained control of eastern Africa, or for that matter, other parts of their far-flung empire, and it is thus worth quoting Hobley extensively here. But for even more detail, see also Piers Brendon's *The Decline and Fall of the British Empire*. (Many of the African tribes in this quotation have been mentioned earlier and are also identified in the map at the end of this chapter; the use of italics and the comments in square brackets are mine):

> "During the early years in Africa (e.g. the nineties of last century [i.e. the 1890's]), it was my privilege to observe closely the process of introducing law and order among a great variety of tribes, and was also myself responsible for bringing a large area under control. ...
>
> The reaction of a native race to control by a civilized Government varies according to their nature, and to their form of government, but in every case a conflict of some kind is inevitable, before the *lower race fully accepts the dictum of the ruling power*. It may come quickly or it may be postponed, but it is often better if it comes quickly. With luck the people may be dealt with in sections, or they may have to be faced as a whole.
>
> In Uganda, which was ruled by a paramount chief supported by a feudal system, the struggle was sectional, and luckily so, for the occupying force was, in the early years, too weak to be really effectual, and it was as much by good fortune as by political ability that Lugard [one of the first British colonialists] avoided submergence. He availed himself of religious feuds, and later on, when that stupid villain Mwanga [whom the explorer Speke had encountered, and whose tyrannical rule might well be viewed as the precursor to that of the much better known Ugandan dictator Idi Amin] threw in his lot with the Sudanese rebels, the Christian chiefs supported us in his

removal from power, so throughout we have always had a strong section of the people on our side. ….

In Kavirondo there was no hegemony as prevailed in Buganda …, but a large collection of small tribes half belonging to the Bantu group, the other half classified as … Nilotic. …….. I found myself in a Bantu section who were generally friendly, but at the same time hoped to enlarge their sphere of influence by the help of the newcomers. It took a long time to unravel the intricate relations of the various tribes in this region and to understand their innumerable blood feuds. ….

So section by section the whole of this great mass became both firm friends and obedient to the law. Still, struggles had to come; *it had to be demonstrated who was master. The component tribes are, however, so virile and responsive, that the solution of the difficulties which arose was a fascinating task, and all along I possessed great faith in the future development of this great collection of people.*

The affairs of the Nandi were quite distinct; they did not kill each other so frequently, but were eternally raiding the Kavirondo, … Looking back, I am convinced that the succession of expeditions was quite avoidable if it had been arranged for the armed forces to have occupied the country for say a couple of years. … the warrior class would soon have come to recognize that they must abandon their traditional way of life….

The Masai presented a separate problem. A great tradition had grown up as to their prowess, and prior to the arrival of British intervention they had undoubtedly held undisputed sway in the centre of Eastern Africa, demanding tribute from every caravan passing through their land. These 'children of the sun' held the convenient theory that all the cattle in the country belonged to them, and they helped themselves to it whenever they thought fit. [It had somehow escaped Hobley's notice that the British held an equally convenient theory that all the administrative right and control over the territory belonged to them.] ...... During the first ten years of Government administration, a custom had grown up of utilizing bodies of Masai to punish a rebellious tribe and they were so employed on the various Nandi expeditions. They were very mobile, for it was their trade, they were skilful at rounding up the enemy's cattle, and their reward was usually one half of the cattle they captured.........

The Kikuyu tribe and its blood relations on the slopes of Mount Kenya are, next to the Kaivorondo, the most numerous native society in Kenya Colony. *They have no internal homogeneity, so were brought under control section by section, without serious military operations.* A perusal of the accounts of the early traders abounds with stories of the treachery of the Kikuyu, and they were rarely exaggerated......... The character of the Kikuyu natives is more complex than that of the Kaivorondo; they are more secretive, more conservative and more difficult to understand. ......

Fifty miles east of Nairobi we find a great tribe called the A-Kamba, which presents many problems. They are, I think, a people of greater mental ability than the Kikuyu, and often exhibit a marked aptitude for mechanical trades. [Another incongruity, since these and other equally gifted tribes are claimed to be the very people incapable of adopting the wheel, perhaps the most simple of mechanical devices.] .... As they have, however, no central organization and owe fealty to no one, each section, jealous of its neighbor and as a rule isolated from it, each community forming an island surrounded by thorn-bush or clustering round a mountain, there was never any fear of serious communal action. Each section gradually accepted Government rule, and when the hut tax was introduced [we will comment on this tax in a later chapter] paid it with little demur. Before our advent, they were harried on the west by the Masai and on the east by the Galla, but held their own fairly well, ...

Only one more tribal group will be referred to, and that is the congery of tribes which inhabit the arid region behind the narrow and fertile coast zone. They are generally termed the Wa-Nikya (the people of the dry bush-land), are cut up in some eight sections, ……. The persistent manner in which they have clung to their ancient beliefs, although they have for several hundred years been in contact with Islam and, during the last fifty years, with Christianity, is a remarkable fact and evidence of either their tenacity of character, or the unreceptive nature of their minds……..

If the decadence of the so-called Swahili, or semi-Arab peoples on the coast continues, it is almost certain that in a few years they will be almost entirely replaced by the flow of Nyika peoples coastwards. Both the descendants of the slave owners and the descendants of the slaves have lost heart. The former have lost their landed property, mortgaging it to Indian merchants in satisfaction of unpaid debts, both ex-masters and ex-slaves living an exiguous existence, and all the coast towns, *except Mombasa,* have greatly decreased in importance, during the last twenty years…… I often think, too, that the coast inhabitants of the lower grades of society, who possessed initiative and enterprise, *drifted up-country with the railway construction,* feeling that there would be more scope for their energies."

One of those enterprising "drifters" moving up-country from the coast with the railway was my pioneering grandfather, of whom we will soon speak.

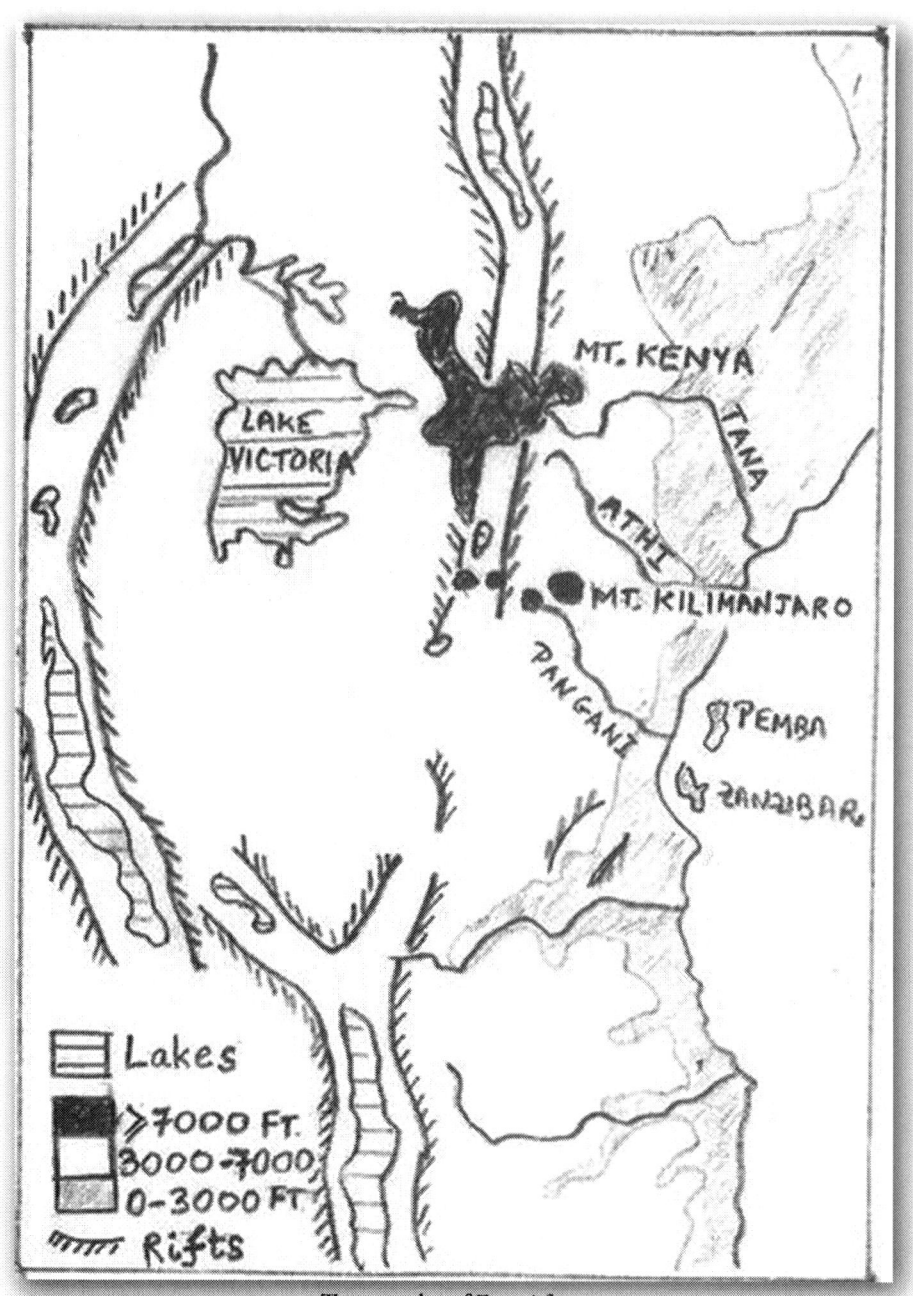

Topography of East Africa

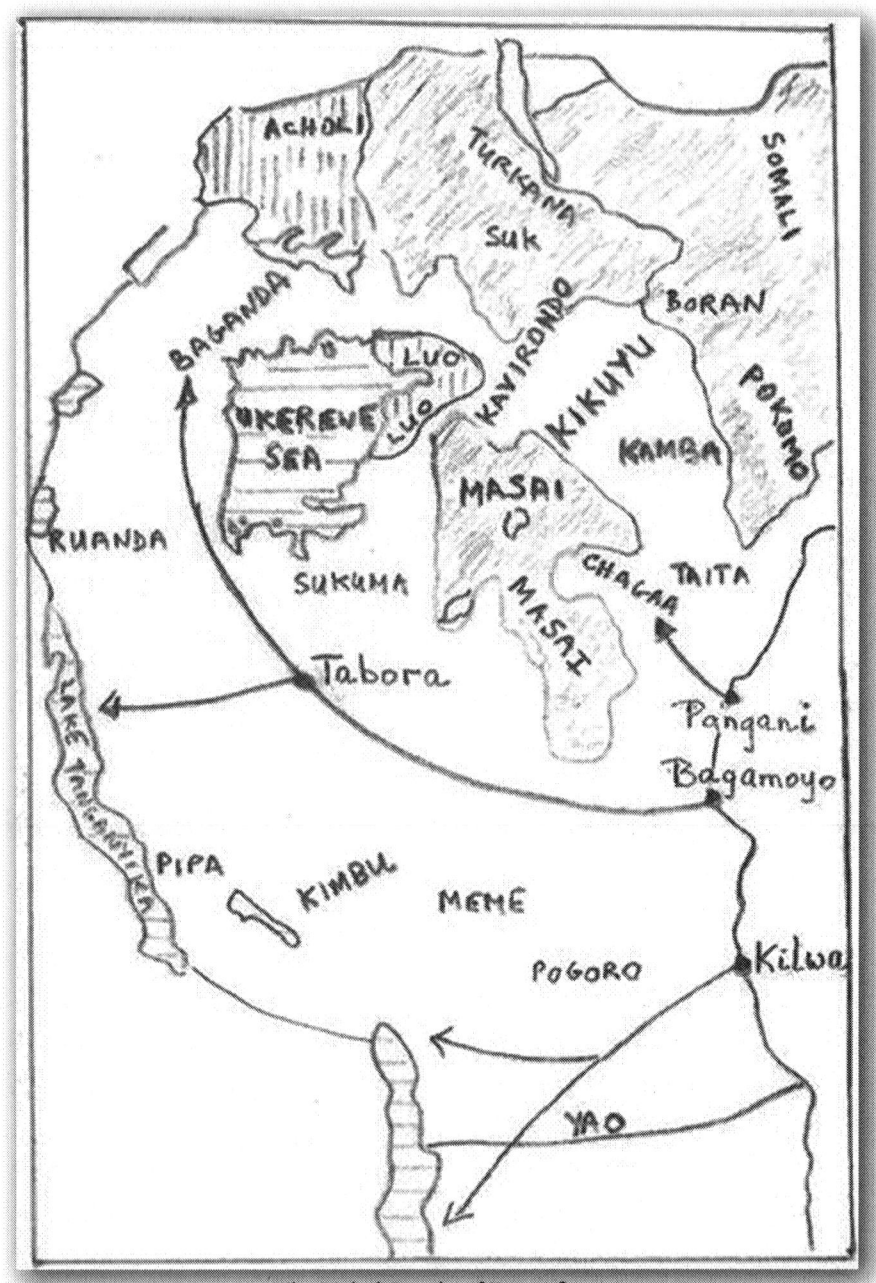

The Tribal People of East Africa

Chapter 3

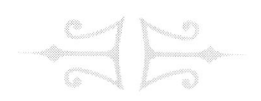

THE LUNATIC LINE

Kenya was born of an intense rivalry for control of East Africa that developed between Great Britain and Germany near the end of the nineteenth century. It hardly seemed to matter to these contestants that a hundred or more African tribes, with highly complex social systems and spoken languages as different as English and Chinese, had vied for this land over the centuries. To use Jared Diamond's apt metaphor for the new form of western political and economic domination, "Guns, Germs, and Steel" would henceforth speak much more loudly than spears, immunity, and stone.

Instead of coming to blows immediately---military confrontation between Britain and Germany was postponed until World War I (WWI) in the next century---the two European nations negotiated and reached an agreement in the so-called 1890 Treaty of Heligoland. This was named for the Atlantic island that Britain handed over to Germany in exchange for the latter relinquishing any claim to the island of Zanzibar, the stepping-stone to the East African mainland. A diagonal line was an agreed boundary, running south-east to north-west from the coast near Zanzibar to the great inland lake named for Queen

Victoria, with a little jog northward to accommodate the snow-capped mountain called Kilimanjaro. Britain's domain lay to the north and Germany's to the south. The hitherto dominant Masai continued to roam freely across this imaginary line in the high plains of East Africa, as they had for centuries. But the consequences for their traditional way of life were soon to become very real.

To gain better control of the territory, the British decided to build a railway from the coast to Lake Victoria. Here lie the headwaters of the Nile river, an area of great strategic importance to Britain, which had already taken charge of Egypt and Sudan, countries to the north for which the river was the lifeblood. There was also a strange idea afloat at the time that the Nile's water supply could be turned off-and-on at the lake like some sort of giant spigot; and an even more bizarre fear, apparently arising from a proposal by a German engineer (who else!) that a drainage canal could be blasted open to drain Lake Victoria into Lake Tanganyika, lying to the south at a lower elevation in the Rift Valley, thereby cutting off the water supply to the Nile. More to the point, the land of the Baganda, bordering on the lake, was rich in potential. It had the capacity to produce a variety of crops for export---cotton, wheat, coffee---and its inhabitants could, in turn, provide a market for British manufactured goods. The scramble for Africa by European powers was ever marked by this strange mix of rationality and irrationality.

A special mystique was associated with the railway during the nineteenth century. Here is what a leading historian and thinker, the late Tony Judt, has to say on the subject, in a soliloquy titled *Ill Fares the Land*:

> "Railways are different. Trains were already the symbol of modern life by the 1840s---hence their appeal to 'modernist' painters from Turner to Monet. They were still performing that role in the age of the great cross-country expresses of the 1890s. Electrified tube trains were the

idols of modernist poets and graphic artist after 1900; nothing was more modern than the new, streamlined super-liners that graced the neo-expressionist posters of the 1930s. The Japanese Shinkansen and French TGV are the very icons of technological wizardry and high comfort at 190 mph today.

Trains, it would seem, are perennially contemporary---even if they slip from sight for a while: in this sense, any country without an efficient rail network is in crucial respects 'backward.' Much the same applies to railway stations. ……..built a century or even a century and a half ago---Paris's Gare l'Est (1852), Paddington Station, London (1854), Budapest's Keleti Palyaudvar (1884), Zurich's Hauptbahnhof (1893)---not only inspire affection: they are aesthetically appealing and they *work*. More to the point, they work in the same way that they did when they were first built. This is a testament to the quality of their design and construction, of course; but it also speaks to their perennial relevance. They do not 'date.'

Stations are not an adjunct to modern life, or part of it, or a by-product of it. Like the railways they punctuate, stations are integral to the modern world itself……"

And thus it was with the creation of a railroad---from the East African coast to a great inland sea---that Kenya came into being and the name "Kenya" became that of a country, not merely the name of a prominent mountain, straddling the equator. The railway line that Britain set out to build in 1895 had meaningful beginning and end points, at the port of Mombasa on the coast and at Port Florence (later renamed Kisumu) on the shores of Lake Victoria, near the fertile kingdom of the dominant Baganda tribe. But otherwise the line would run through a no-man's land that was largely unchartered at the time. Long before it was completed at vast expense, it came to be known as the "lunatic line." (The original estimate of its cost was three and a half million British pounds, an enormous sum in those days, and a figure that eventually doubled.) The African tribes whose territory was being encroached upon, in particular the Kikuyu, had a very different name for the railway line. They called it the "iron snake," demonstrating a good understanding of its poisonous implications for their future.

An earlier attempt at building a narrow-gauge railway from Mombasa had been made by the Imperial British East Africa Company (IBEAC), which held a charter to the territory before it became a British Protectorate. One of the early pioneering officials in Kenya, the remarkable Charles Hobley mentioned in the previous chapter, was assigned a variety of responsibilities by the IBEAC, and later the Colonial Office. In his memoir, he recalls the following episode, which would be hilarious if it were not so tragic:

"I was at that time in charge of the earthworks division, and near the point at which the line reached the Changamwe plateau [near Mombasa] a considerable embankment crossed a gully, and this was constructed in the usual African or Indian method, by streams of men tipping earth carried in small baskets. One day its height reached the survey level, and the rails were laid across it in order that it might be widened by means of side tip-trucks. As fate would have it, a day or two later there took place the trial run of the first locomotive, which had been assembled in the workshops on the Point. The head fitter, a man named Futter, was rather proud of his achievement, and successfully drove it up the steep incline to the plateau. When he approached my embankment he conceived the rash idea of rushing across it; it was, of course, soft and unsettled, and consequently gave way, the engine turning a complete somersault. The wretched Futter was picked up with his back badly damaged, and he died a few days later. This was my first experience of railway construction, and rather disturbing for a youngster."

Poor Futter! As the old aphorism goes, the world is a comedy to those who think and a tragedy to those who feel. If Hobley were given to expressing himself in the form of a limerick instead of in prose, he may well have written instead:

> "There was an old fitter named Futter
> Who used to put bread *on* his butter
> So 'twas no great surprise
> That he met his demise
> Somersaulting his cab in a gutter."

The IBEAC effort was still-born and abandoned after the railway had penetrated only a few miles inland. Soon thereafter, Hobley was assigned to an expedition sent to explore and map the Tana river in northern Kenya, the only major navigable river in the country and viewed as a potential artery for opening up the interior. The exploration, initiated in March, 1891, was undertaken by a stern-wheel steamer, appropriately named the *Kenya*, which was shipped to Mombasa from Britain in bits and pieces and reassembled for the voyage of exploration, a journey that Hobley described in his memoir in vivid detail.

The first fifteen miles of his journey, where the river paralleled the coast, went through gloomy mangrove swamp that formed an impenetrable wall on either side, with the roar of the ocean breakers in the distance. For the next one hundred miles or so, Hobley found the countryside rather uninspiring and the river banks relatively barren and untimbered. But then the scenery changed dramatically, and for the next hundred he discovered unbroken forest of striking beauty, enhanced by a wealth of bird life: pelicans, cranes, herons of every kind, duck and teal. However, navigation was difficult because of floating logs and other vegetation that snagged the rudder and the underside of the vessel. Eventually waterfalls and rapids were encountered, which prevented further progress by steamer, and Hobley disembarked to lead a team that continued its explorations on foot. They followed the Tana river westwards on an arc south of Mount Kenya and after many adventures eventually returned by an inland route to Mombasa, where Hobley had been given up for lost. His recollections of this remarkable 1891-92 journey, first published in a memoir in 1929, are fascinating in their entirety, but the paragraphs that I found the most compelling are the following (italics mine):

"The Tana is a miniature Nile, and its valley is potentially the richest portion of Kenya Colony; the river brings down an enormous quantity of silt per annum, and at flood-time the chocolate-coloured mud tinges the water far out to sea. For many miles of its lower course the river has, like many others, a natural levee, which means that its flood plain is below the level of the river, and this would greatly facilitate irrigation.

Of course this vast alluvial plain cannot be considered healthy enough for European settlement, but that is not the reason for its neglect; it is mainly due to the fact that it is thinly populated by a primitive people, who have neither the knowledge nor the energy to make the best use of their habitat.

This state of affairs cannot continue indefinitely, and I believe that it is no rash prophecy to state that, in the near future, some immigration scheme will be considered by which this great area can be peopled by a race who understand how to use irrigation water, and above all realize that it will pay to buy it. *It will then produce rice, cotton and sugar in vast quantities for the use of the world.*

At a very conservative estimate, we have here some 20,000 square miles of irrigable land of unlimited fertility waiting for cultivation. The Pokomo, dotted about in little villages over about 300 miles of the course of the river, only number 15,000, if as many, and only collectively occupy a few square miles of territory. *With properly conceived works, there is no reason why this area should not accommodate, eventually, a population of a million souls.* Would that more could see this fine river at flood-time, roaring by with its chocolate-coloured burden of fertilizing material, all going to waste!."

This quotation is striking on several fronts and especially because it shows the different mindset of the newest arrivals to the African continent. The inhabitants of the Tana region at that time, the Pokomo tribe mentioned in the foregoing quotation, are described by Hobley as "curious folk" whose lives were so interwoven with the river as to make them almost amphibious. They had a particular relish for the flesh of a fellow amphibian, the crocodile, which they feared little and hunted almost to extinction; and, when the river flooded, they supplemented their diet by growing a little rice of excellent quality. The "immigration scheme" Hobley had in mind was perhaps to bring in Egyptians or Sudanese workers who were familiar with exploiting the silt and floodwaters of the Nile, or even southern Indians for whom rice was a staple. But this scheme came of nought. Hobley's prophecy did indeed prove to be "rash," and the type of development he had envisioned for the Tana floodplain never took place. Soon after his journey of exploration, Britain chose to back a horse of a very different color---the "iron" horse---and simultaneously to adopt a very different immigration policy from that advocated by Hobley.

Initially, a cart road was commissioned, the construction being spearheaded by a Captain Sclater for whom it was eventually named. This road roughly paralleled the route envisioned for the railway and helped supply the workers during the period of the railroad construction, between 1895 and 1901, and it could easily have been adapted to the needs of the soon-to-arrive automobile. But once the railway line from Mombasa to Lake Victoria was complete, Slater's cart road and the Tana

River way of Hobley's imagination were both cast aside in favor of the railroad---its enormous investment of capital had to be recovered---and the development of Kenya Colony proceeded accordingly.

When the Ugandan railway was commissioned, steam engine and railroad technology, which originated with James Watt in 1775 (a year before the American Revolution!) were already well developed. Railways, as recounted above, had been constructed in many countries. In India, the "jewel in the crown" of the British Empire, to which the British turned their attention after their ejection from North America, an extensive network of railway lines had been built. And following the American Civil War, the construction of a railway line across the United States was completed. Think of what it involved in crossing the Rocky Mountains and the High Sierras! Perhaps an even greater feat was the construction of the trans-Canadian railroad, spearheaded by William Van Horne, and completed in 1885. Of this effort, Piers Brendon writes:

> "...the Canadian Pacific Railway (CPR) embarked on its titanic struggle with the forces of nature. The first great barrier was the Canadian Shield itself, the pre-Cambrian carapace of gneiss and granite that stretched down to the tempestuous shores of Lake Superior. The earth's most ancient armour, this hard, grey, ridged rock presented Van Horne with '200 miles of engineering impossibilities.' For months his men blasted their way through it using three tons of dynamite a day and causing many fatal accidents. Next they faced a three-hundred-mile tract of sphagnum bog, guarded by walls of black flies and mosquitoes which ... made the insects of India seem almost benign. .... Next came the prairie, an arid expanse white with buffalo bones.... Every stick, plank, sleeper and telegraph pole had to be hauled from Winnipeg into this 850-mile-wide steppe .... So did every rail, spike, fish plate and load of provisions---a logistical operation

to baffle any general. But assembly-line organization caused the steel to roll westwards at *nearly three and a half miles each day.* …..[Then Van Horne] strove to thread his way through the monstrous cordillera. … The route….was serpentine, precipitous and choked by icy jungle. ….. Many workers perished during the final push, including a disproportionate number of Chinese. Tradition has it that every foot of railroad built through the Fraser Canyon cost a coolie's life…."

Compared to these efforts, the building of the Ugandan railway---roughly 600 miles in length and a matter of transferring a well-developed and proven technology to the new environment---seems relatively straightforward. In East Africa, a desert known as the Nyika, which bordered the coastal plain, and the Great Rift Valley, in the central part of the country, both presented formidable obstacles. But they were as nothing compared to the topography encountered in North America, and, analogous to the use of Chinese labor in America, the task of construction could be facilitated by importing Indian "coolies" who were already conversant with railways on the subcontinent.

All the same, the Mombasa-Kisumu railway did pose new and unique challenges. When railway construction was undertaken in India and North America, the territories had already been wrested away from their original inhabitants by European incursion, over decades if not centuries. Thus they were already well explored, with numerous settlements along the way to facilitate transportation and for the provisioning of food and water. But this was far from the case with the construction of the Ugandan railroad. Its history is nicely summarized by Patrick Pringle in a little booklet titled *The Story of a Railway*, and, in particular, he notes the lack of the most basic forms of animal transport, which were tried without success, for reasons noted in the previous chapter. (Both camels and horses died quickly, and bullocks could not be used because of the lack of water and disease-carrying tsetse flies.) Donkeys were almost the only animals that could be used, and they were difficult to obtain. So transport beyond the railhead was done by human porters. The existing caravan infrastructure as described in the previous chapter proved to be invaluable and it operated in tandem with the construction of the railway, thereby achieving astonishing results. For example, Pringle notes the following:

> "The first steamer launched on [Lake] Victoria Nyanza was the *Kenya*. She was carried from the coast in sections, in 1896. The railway took the sections as far as it went, and the journey was completed by porters. They went over the Uasin Gishu Plateau, and scores of plates and other important parts were dropped and lost in the long grass. There was a long delay before fresh parts were brought and the sections were put together and the steamer launched.
>
> The 62-ton steamboat *William Mackinnon* was taken in the same way, and launched in June 1900. The two bigger steamers, the *Winifred* and *Sybil*, were built and taken to the lake. By the time the railway was finished, these and other steamboats were running regularly between Port Florence and Entebbe and other lake ports."

The aforementioned *Kenya* was very likely the same steamboat that took Charles Hobley on his voyage of discovery along the Tana River, the boat having been disassembled and then reassembled for a second time. The *Kenya*, steaming across Lake Victoria, must have been a sad symbol of the Tana riverway that *might have been*. In an ironic twist of fate, it had succumbed to the very railway that was used to transport the disassembled steamboat to the lake.

For the railroad construction workers, disease was a constant hazard: malaria, plague, cholera, and the sickness brought on by a parasite carried by the tsetse fly. The latter was unique to Africa, a pernicious insect that John Gunter describes in vivid terms in his 1950's travelogue:

"The fly is medium-sized, and lives on only one commodity---blood. It breeds by preference in shady thickets, and has a comparatively short range of flight, but is swift. It looks very much like the fly one sees in temperate climates around barns, but it can easily be distinguished from ordinary flies by the fact that its wings do not project sideways, but overlap crosswise on the back. Its bite is sharp and painful---a deep, blood-sucking stab. But the tsetse fly, even though it is one of the most damaging creatures in the world, is not the real villain. It does not cause trypanosomiasis, but merely carries it. The real villain is a trypanosome, or parasite, which lives in the bloodstreams of various beasts---lions, zebras, buffaloes, antelopes, even frogs and crocodiles. These animals are hosts to the trypanosome, but are immune to it. When the fly bites an infected beast, it may spread the disease if it subsequently bites another beast [or human] not immune. Domestic cattle are not immune and therefore cannot exist healthily in fly-infested territory. ....

More than four *million* square miles of Africa are 'under the fly', an area much bigger than the whole United States; the fly belt stretches all the way across Africa from the Sudan to the Union [of South Africa], brushing both coasts. This does not mean that every nook and cranny of this Brobdingnagian block of territory is contaminated; if that were so life would cease on the African continent. But very large areas *are* contaminated at least to the extent that cattle cannot be freely grazed."

Other hazards for railway workers were also unique to East Africa. The tiny "chigger," or jigger, burrowed into bare feet, usually near a toenail, and deposited a sac of eggs. If not extracted skillfully with a sterilized needle and the site disinfected with carbolic acid, it would lead to ulceration or gangrene, and eventually to the amputation of infected toes. At the other end of the spectrum of animal hazards, less-than-tiny lions imposed a reign of terror that at one point brought a complete cessation of work on the railroad. These man-eaters were so difficult to shoot or poison that the workers came to believe that they were not animals at all, but evil spirits in the form of lions. Altogether they killed and ate twenty-eight Indian coolies and many more Africans, before they were finally shot. (A full accounting can be found in Colonel Patterson's *The Man-Eaters of Tsavo*.) And, of course, the weather governed by the monsoon winds on the equatorial belt created enormous problems: heavy rains during the wet season washed away miles of track, and, during the dry season, drought conditions would lead to a great shortage of potable water.

But disease and obstacles notwithstanding, the railhead reached mile 326 on May 30, 1899, a conveniently flat area with a water supply from a nearby river, and here on the plain where previously nothing stood, the city of Nairobi began to sprout and grow. A rare photograph, dated circa 1900, reveals a fine, well-constructed railway station---the type that Tony Judt had celebrated---along with some railway sheds, but all looking out to *an entirely empty plain.*

Chapter 4

MY PIONEERING GRANDFATHER

Usually new settlement precedes the construction of a railway, as was the case with the North American continent. In Kenya it was just the opposite. White settlers from South Africa, Great Britain, and other parts of continental Europe were actively recruited and began to flow upcountry, following and spreading out from the railway route. So did Indians from the subcontinent, with their little shops, called *dukas*, and their business horse sense, just as they had settled for centuries along the more ancient human caravan routes to the south, albeit in smaller numbers. Although most of the approximately 30,000 Indian laborers imported to work on the railway had returned to India---roughly 2500 died and about 7000 remained in Kenya---a fresh wave of immigrants from India then began to arrive and among them were my grandfather, Joachim Antonio, and his family.

According to family lore, my grandfather came to Kenya from India by dhow, the centuries-old sailing transport on the "monsoon highway." He was brought out by his brother, R.A. Nazareth, who was a railway clerk, but the precise date of his arrival at the end of the 19th century is unclear. My grandfather was an adventurous man of forceful character and endowed with considerable organizational skill, and he rose from humble beginnings. He started out in Kenya with little knowledge of the English language and began work in a kitchen, but he was soon able to attain considerable prosperity, a tale that harkens back to the classic American immigrant story. To get some sense of his adventurous beginning on the Kenyan frontier, think of an immigrant to a state like Arizona in the American West, at the beginning of the twentieth century. Its capital Phoenix, today a thriving city akin to present-day Nairobi, was then little more than a row of shacks on a railway line that branched westward to California. If only my grandfather had kept a diary, a chronicle of mundane, day-to-day events! It could have been transmuted into story-tellers' gold by the wand of time. Now, one can only get a sense of his particular circumstances and colorful journey---build a *verbal collage* of extracts as we shall below---from the published accounts of other early pioneers and historians of that period, and from the travelogues of adventurers who came to East Africa at a later date. For example, John Gunther, a peripatetic traveler and author of several travel books spanning four continents, visited Zanzibar in the 1950s and describes it as follows:

> "This is one of the most enticing little domains left in the world---an island some twenty miles off the East African coast near the Equator. The name comes from the Persian *zenj* (black) and means 'Country of the Blacks'. But nowadays Zanzibar is not so much black as a mixture of various browns. It lives mostly on cloves, and the island is permeated by their aromatic scent. The streets are narrow, dark, and almost vaulted; the houses still have massive teakwood doors, delicately carved and studded with huge brass buttons. Zanzibar is, on the surface, largely an Arab town. It gives a note of secrecy, moistness,

and dilapidation. …. Next to the configuration of the town itself, the most romantic thing about Zanzibar is the long line of dhows in the harbor. These ships, some of which displace four hundred tons or more, are propelled entirely by sail. The dhow traffic depends, of course, on the monsoons, which are as regular as metronomes. … Sometimes as many as three hundred dhows are parked in Zanzibar between monsoons."

That is the world my grandfather would have experienced had the dhow on which he travelled arrived at Zanzibar harbor rather than Mombasa. Family lore again holds that after arriving at Mombasa he then traversed much of the three-hundred mile journey from the coast to Nairobi on foot, and, although apocryphal in nature, there is likely some truth to this tale, because the railway line at that time was only partially complete and may not have reached mile 326. Even if he had travelled from Mombasa to Nairobi entirely by train, the thirty-six hour journey was far from safe or comfortable. It was not uncommon for passengers to have to hop out and put their shoulders to a wheezing engine to help it up a steep incline---Nairobi was at 5,000 feet above sea level---and sometimes, perhaps when the complement of passengers was not of a particularly sturdy nature, the only solution was to send back to Mombasa for a supplementary engine. On one occasion it is reported that a train was considerably delayed because its steam-engine's boiler had been punctured by a charging rhino. And as Errol Trzebinski reports in her book *The Kenya Pioneers*, "plagues of army worm---which appeared after periods of drought---would impede progress when their tiny bodies were crushed against the line, making it so slippery that the wheels lost their grip." But there were also rewards to the journey. A wonderful sense of comraderie would develop between the passengers, who made themselves comfortable with spirit lamps for brewing tea or coffee, picnic baskets, whisky, and tobacco. People were allowed to bring their most unusual pets on board: monkeys, young gazelle, hyrax, mongooses, sometimes even tame baby leopards or lions. And outside, on the Athi plains through which the train passed, animals teemed as far as the eye could see, a moving mass of wildebeest, zebra, Thomson's gazelle, reedbuck, duiker and other small antelope, stately giraffe and flocks of ostriches, black rhinos dozing beneath the thorn trees, a herd of elephants in the distance, not to mention the large and small cats, ever-present but usually hidden from view in the tall grasses. As late as 1910, when ex-President Teddy Roosevelt traveled on this train during a sight-seeing visit to Kenya, he described it as a "journey through the Pleistocene."

One of my favorite memoirs from that time was penned by the rapscallion John Boyes and immodestly titled *King of the Wa-Kikuyu*, the King being himself, of course. He describes adventures in Kenya during the period 1898-1901, which overlapped with my grandfather's arrival. Kikuyuland was then fractured amongst many tribes that were constantly at odds with one another, and Boyes, by dint of personality, had managed to place himself at the head of one of the major warring factions. In his memoir he recounts the following:

> "...rumour reached me that three Goanese [immigrants from Portuguese Goa] had been murdered and all their safari wiped out. I gathered that it was a trading safari that had started out from Nairobi, headed by three Goanese, who had with them about forty Kikuyu natives....... They had entered the Kikuyu country, and had been well treated by the natives whom I had got under control, having a really good time until they had entered the Chinga country. The Goanese had, perhaps, not reckoned on the other natives being different, and consequently had not taken proper precautions. They were well armed---about fifteen of the natives carrying rifles, besides themselves, but in spite of this the Chinga people had for some reason

attacked and murdered the whole party. ….. From what I could make out there must have been thousands of natives in the business, and they had completely wiped out the traders' safari and taken everything that they possessed---trade goods, some cattle they had with them, and everything that was worth looting."

John Boyes, in his role as "King," then initiated a prolonged fight between his Kikuyu allies and the Chinga people, in which the latter were completely routed. He describes this conflict and then continues as follows (italics mine):

"The trouble being thus settled, …. I had complete control of the country; everything that had been stolen from the Goanese had been given up, while their murderers had received such punishment as they were not likely to forget in a generation.

When matters had quieted down again, and I had time to review the situation, I took the first opportunity of sending messengers through to the government, with a full report of the recent occurrences; *while I also communicated with the relatives of the murdered Goanese, two brothers who, I heard, were living at Nairobi,* sending through to them the whole of the stolen property which I had recovered. I found out later that, through some misunderstanding, or other, the heads of the murdered men---which had been found after the fighting was over---had likewise been sent to Nairobi; which, while serving as proof to the officials that the reports I had been sending in from time to time as to the character of the natives were not without foundation, was of most regrettable occurrence, and must, I fear, have given much pain to the relatives."

These events took place around 1900-1901 and while it is unlikely that my grandfather and his brother in Nairobi were the two brothers mentioned in the above narrative, it is very likely that they were well acquainted with the murdered Goans of this unfortunate safari.

By the year 1903, my grandfather and his brother had become well established and were making their presence felt in their newly adopted country. For example, Errol Trzebinski's *The Kenya Pioneers* contains the following amusing description of the train journey, in April, 1903, of one Abraham Block, a Jewish immigrant from Lithuania, which sheds light on my grandfather's business activities (italics mine):

> "Most Europeans automatically travelled first-class unlike Block who could only afford a second-class ticket. The old Indian coaches had no corridor, and were referred to as 'the loose boxes' or 'horse boxes'. Each compartment slept four, the bunks lying parallel to the track so that progress was animated by a ceaseless jolting action only to be relieved by the halts made for meals. These were served in '*dak*' bungalows where *the catering was under contract to a Goan, Mr. J. Nazareth.* Block, being more familiar with the necessities of life than the luxuries, thought the standard of food was good and happily paid one rupee for lunch and dinner and fifty-five annas for his breakfast of hardboiled eggs and tea. But his opinion was an exception. Generally newcomers were startled by Nazareth's menu which seldom varied from watery soup, tinned salmon, meat balls and fruit and custard. More puzzling still was the nostalgia the railway meals summoned in the old hands, who appeared to find comfort in their awfulness. It was something to do with being back where they belonged. Dinner was served by Goan stewards in white gloves as multitudes of winged insects, attracted to the lamps suspended like low billiard lights over each table, slid down the shades into the soup or lodged themselves in the butter."

Tinned food was brought to East Africa for the first time by American engineers, who had done much of the steelwork on the railway, and no doubt it was by this means that my grandfather was able to secure an ample supply of tinned (canned) salmon. I've often wondered at my own father's predilection for foods on the railway menu, which probably came from my grandfather serving the same menu in his "dak" railway bungalows and at his dining table at home. And, if truth be told, I must admit to a special fondness for tinned salmon, and watery soup as well.

The aforementioned Abraham Block did very well for himself in the rapidly developing colony. (With his two sons, he eventually created Block Hotels, the largest hotel chain in Kenya.) So did my grandfather and his brother, and by 1908, the year of my father's birth, they had attained considerable prosperity. They ran a well-known firm, Nazareth Bros., and in their days of affluence, they owned a shop, a bar, a hotel, and as noted in the above quote, they also had the railway catering contract. For example, in *A Railway Runs Through*, Selma Carvalho notes the following:

> "The Nazareth brothers had displayed their gumption and their 'unbounded faith in the town of Nairobi' by erecting so 'fine a building' on Government Road and opening a sumptuous store. Inside the store, was a cornucopia of delightful items: a well-stocked haberdashery, *sola topees* [pith helmets; also called sun hats], boots, shoes, delicacies of all kinds, fresh tobacco, soft blankets and fine fabrics, jewellery, crockery, glassware and the latest novels. Women were spared from having to deal with brusque male salesmen; the ladies department was under the management of a European lady. A 'good assortment of English papers and magazines was received on every mail'. The old store was converted into a restaurant; four rooms fronting the road were set aside as dining rooms reserved for Europeans, with an adjoining billiard room."

And again:

> The Nazareth brothers took daring risks at a time when Nairobi's future was bleak and ambiguous at best, when capital infusions and faith in the fumbling protectorate were both in scarce supply. Among their significant business ventures was a soda-water factory operated by Hayward & Tyler machinery and with the capacity to produce 150 dozens of soda-water bottles per day."

My granduncle became a member of the Nairobi Town Council, defeating in the election Dr. R. A. Ribeiro, Nairobi's first doctor. Errol Trzebinski describes this extraordinary, pioneering figure in Kenya's history as follows (italics mine):

> "In February 1900, Dr Rosendo Ayres Ribeiro, Nairobi's first private medical practitioner, made his appearance. His tubby, Goanese figure became familiar as he *rode his tame zebra* about the Bazaar or along Station Road. He pitched his tent where the bakery later stood on Whitehouse Road. Wearing a Stetson, his black beard trimmed neatly, his buttons looking as if they would pop off his waistcoat at any moment, Dr. Ribeiro visited the sick among all the communities. He became famous in Nairobi for his special malarial cure, which he patented and was sold to an international pharmaceutical company eventually. For six months he and his assistant, Mr. C. Pinto, shared a tent as home and practice. In the evenings, by the light of a candle and a kerosene lamp they made up prescriptions of the young Goanese doctor's invention. He cured many grateful settlers of fever with his nameless, grey powders; the first dose induced vomiting which produced a lot of green bile but that was the extent of the discomfort. After completing the course his patients were assured of freedom from fever for many months.

> As the Indian Bazaar expanded Dr Ribeiro moved into more luxurious quarters and their next surgery was built from packing cases in which his drug supplies were shipped from England. A tarpaulin, borrowed from the railway, provided the temporary cover and when it was reclaimed he practiced under no roof, like Aesculapius in the Sacred Groves, receiving many a tough native chicken in lieu of payment for his cures. It was Dr. Ribeiro who, in 1902, had diagnosed bubonic plague in two Somali patients and reported it."

At this point, it is best to pick up the story from the memoir of Charles Hobley:

"One day, news came from Nairobi of a serious outbreak of plague in the Indian Bazaar, and the P.M.O. [Principal Medical Officer, a European] was summoned from Mombasa to investigate it. He was, according to modern ideas, an ignorant leech, but a man of very emphatic opinions, so he walked through the bazaar and with Napoleonic decision ordered it to be burned down, lock, stock and barrel. This was done and a nice sum it cost the Government for compensation. After this dramatic incident, general orders were issued to take measures to prevent the spread of plague along the railway line."

And now returning once again to Errol Trzebinski:

"Dr. Ribeiro's surgery went up with the rest. This drastic measure cost the Government 50,000 pounds [the 'nice sum' mentioned above] but Dr. Ribeiro fared rather well out of the disaster. He was compensated for the loss with the gift of a domestic plot near the station. There he built the usual *Dak* bungalow on stilts, from which he carried on his work and, in 1903, was given a concession of sixteen acres behind Victoria Street by the Government in recognition for services rendered over his report on the plague."

Other equally outstanding figures in Kenya's early days, in particular immigrants of British origin, are writ large in the pages of Trzebinski's *The Kenya Pioneers*. And for the parallel story of pioneers of Indian origin, see *A History of Asians in East Africa c. 1866 to 1945* by J.S. Mangat. Amongst them, perhaps the most remarkable of all is Allidina Visram, who began as a small trader along the caravan routes in the 1880s and built an extensive commercial network of small shops, or *dukas*, and other business interests spanning all of East Africa. In the Nile district, in particular, he became known as the "uncrowned King of Uganda" and not self-proclaimed as was the case with John Boyes. In addition to his dukas, his interests included furniture-making in Kampala and Entebbe, soda factories, oil mills at Kisumu and at the coast, a soap factory at Mombasa, cotton-ginning establishments at Mombasa and Entebbe, saw-mills in Uganda and Kenya, a small steamboat and a fleet of sailing vessels on Lake Victoria. Revered by his fellow Indian businessmen, who often got a start in one of his enterprises, by the Government to which he rendered valuable services in the early days, and by the public at large for his philanthropic activities--- including significant donations to schools, a hospital, and religious establishments---his death in 1916, in the middle of WWI, was mourned by all. And its aftermath is described by Mangat as follows:

> "But the entrepreneurial skills which enabled Allidina Visram to play such an important role in the economic history of East Africa are necessarily qualities in short supply. His son and successor, A.A. Visram, continued to operate the extensive business network he had inherited, and the firm's predominance in the commercial life of Uganda and to a lesser extent of Kenya and Tanganyika was to continue. But shortly

after the latter's death in 1923, Allidina Visram's remarkable business empire rapidly disintegrated. In 1918 his estate was worth well over Rs. 3 million [an enormous sum in those days]; by 1925 his successors had become 'practically penniless' and sought the Government's assistance on the strength of Allidina's services to the Administration in the early days. …. Finally in 1926 the creditors of A.A. Visram's bankrupt estate had to content themselves with the payment of a mere 2 per cent dividend. However, a few streets in a number of East African towns named after Allidina Visram, or his statue at Mombasa (which was recently removed), act as reminders of his commercial ventures ……."

Likewise, in what turned out to be a parallel story, albeit on a much smaller scale, my grandfather's fortune and his family continued to grow in the years preceding WWI. His eldest daughter Natividad---the Aunty Nathu of whom we have spoken in a previous chapter---was the only child born in Indo-Portuguese Goa, before my grandmother joined my grandfather in British East Africa. Their other seven children were born in Nairobi, my father, John Maximian, being the third son and fourth child. He arrived in 1908 in the heart of the Indian section of the town, on River Road, in a wood-and-iron house, so-called because it was built from wood and roofed with sheets of corrugated iron. One of his earliest recollections was that of being "dangerously ill with typhoid in a one-room upper storey and being tended by a European nurse"---a testament to the unsanitary nature of Nairobi's water supply in those early days and also to the considerable prosperity that my paternal grandfather had already attained.

By coincidence, electricity first came to Nairobi in the very year of my father's birth. Turbo-generators set up at a dam on the nearby Ruiru River supplied the power, and by 1910 the streets of the rapidly-growing town, itself barely ten years of age, were illuminated by electric light. One night soon afterwards, it is recorded that the street lights of Nairobi flickered and dimmed over a period of many hours until the cause was identified: a hippopotamus had managed to enter the wooden flumes that supplied water to the generators and got stuck within, impeding the flow.

Schools in Nairobi at that time were primitive and initially organized by the railway authorities. In 1907, a year before my father's birth, there were two such schools under the joint control of a European headmaster, one with forty-six Indian students and the other with forty Europeans. These were both taken over by the government in 1910, and thereafter, with the help of government grants, the Indian and European immigrants organized their own schools along communal and religious lines. African schools, aside from rudimentary education provided by the Christian missions, were practically nonexistent. My father spent a few months in the Catholic Parochial School located near Nairobi's present-day Catholic Cathedral, where he recalls "of those school days I retain but a faint memory. I am told I could at times be a difficult child, apt sometimes even to kick the nuns if they went, I thought, too far." In the interests of providing the children with a better education, the whole family, with the exception of my grandfather, left for India in 1913. It was a prescient decision on the part of my grandparents, because the First World War (WWI) was soon to engulf Europe, with dramatic consequences for neighboring German Tanganyika, which thereafter fell to Great Britain, a fresh addition to the British Empire.

Business continued to go well for my grandfather up to the beginning of World War I and one can find another amusing passage on his activities in Lord Cransworth's *Kenya Chronicles* (italics again mine):

"On March 21st, the line of the Ruwu being firmly held, the forces to which I was attached were moved back to Mbuyuni, a comparatively dry and healthy camp, to be reorganized and brought up to strength to resume active operations at the end of the rains. Major-General A.R. Hoskins was brought in to command the 1st Division, which was our official name, and I made his acquaintance in an unfortunate fashion in which I very rightly incurred his severe displeasure. My friend Colin Isaacson was acting as D.A.Q.M.G. and I had occasion to go down to his office. He was not in and I took the opportunity for some ill-placed facetiousness. This was the time when almost all civilians were presented with military titles, and among others the head of the Y.M.C.A. store had been gazetted a Major. *The only other store in the camp was run by a large Goan, with long yellow Dundreary whiskers, named Nazareth.* I took a sheet of official paper and wrote to Colin in official terms. I stated that in the Major's store I had found neither soap nor toilet paper but proceeding had found ample supplies provided by the Goan. Under the circumstances I put forward the suggestion that Nazareth should be promoted to Brigadier-General, which I further pointed out would be a graceful compliment to our oldest ally. This I left in an official envelope and went on my way. Shortly the newly arrived General visited his H.Q. office and opened the envelope addressed to his D.A.Q.M.G. The fat was in the fire. I was sent for, properly told off, and told that he would take twenty-four hours to consider whether or not to send me back to the base. I spent a miserable day and night, and the following afternoon an orderly brought an official envelope. I tore it open in fear and trembling to read: *"I have seen Nazareth. You are forgiven. He should be a General. Come to dinner tonight."* I have never been facetious on office paper again. General Hoskins was perhaps the most gifted soldier of the campaign and was certainly the most popular."

But, sometime during this period, things went very wrong. My grandfather and his brother lost their entire fortune and were forced to declare bankruptcy. In his memoir, *Brown Man Black Country,* my father traces this misfortune to the large amount of bad debt that my grandfather accumulated from British officers and soldiers during the War, pilfering by staff, borrowing from money-lenders at exorbitant rates of interest, and possibly the conduct of business at times when he was the worse off for drink---in short, irresponsible business habits. Family lore, again most likely exaggerated, holds that my grandfather gave away his hotel, in particular, for a kiss.

Very little is known about my grandfather's life after he lost his fortune and was reduced to penury. There is a donated soccer trophy, called the Nazareth Cup, for which soccer teams in Kenya competed annually for many years after his death. And there is his fine headstone in the Forest Road Cemetery. But more than anything else he left a son, my father, of whom he is reported to have said shortly before his death: "Mackie will make my name." And, as we shall soon see, indeed Mackie did.

My Paternal Grandfather, Joachim Antonio Nazareth

Chapter 5

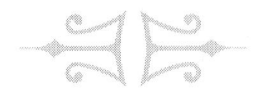

GOLDEN GOA TURNED TO CLAY

When my paternal grandmother traveled with her children to British India in 1913, just before the commencement of World War I, her two eldest sons were enrolled as boarders at St. Mary's High School in Bombay, today's bustling and energetic Mumbai, but at that time a much more leisurely colonial city. She and her other children, including my father, then returned to Goa, the small remaining fragment of Portugal's long-lost empire, from whence my grandparents had emigrated to Kenya at the end of the 19th century. There they resumed residence temporarily in the house that my grandfather had retained in his ancestral village of Moira, in the northern province of Goa called Bardez.

Goa, located on the western coast of India about 300 miles south of Mumbai, is postage-stamp sized, approximately 60 miles in length from north to south, and about 30 miles wide. With the ocean to the west, a dominant river system bisecting the territory into northern and southern regions, and a broad estuary with a fine harbor on which its principal city is located, the former colony is like a scaled-down version of Portugal itself, the latter being a little more rectangular in shape. From north to south, Portugal is about six times longer than Goa, and like Goa about half as wide as it is long. To Portugal's west lies the Atlantic Ocean, into which flows the river Tejo, roughly bisecting the country and opening into a wide estuary, the harbor for the capitol city of Lisbon. In the case of Goa, the corresponding estuary is created by the convergence of two main rivers, the Mandovi and the Zuari, which define the northern and southern boundaries of a large island between them, the Isle of Goa. To the north is the province known as Bardez, where the village of Moira and my paternal grandparents' ancestral home were located, and to the south the province known as Salsette. Much of the history of Portuguese Goa centered on the Isle and these two provinces.

The western boundary of Goa is defined by the Indian Ocean, where the string of beaches for which the state has been famous over the centuries are located, and the eastern boundary is formed by a rib of mountains called the Ghats, where the westward-flowing rivers originate. Goa's principal town Panjim, today's Panaji, lies near the excellent harbor and in the early 20th century it served as the colony's administrative center. But the bulk of Goa's residents continued to live in villages like Moira---small, self-contained "republics," where farming was often done in rural cooperatives and the village church or temple served as a community center---whose number exceeded three hundred. From these villages, they commuted to the main towns or made a living locally within an agriculture-based economy.

When my grandparents emigrated in the late 1890s, Goa was at a nadir. Like Portugal of that time, the little colony on the Indian subcontinent was haunted by the echoes and ghosts of an earlier golden age and offered little hope of advancement to men of ambition. Goans had left in droves after the mid-19th century in search of better opportunities in British India and farther afield. But, nevertheless, emigrants like my grandparents had preserved, and indeed cherished, the connection with their ancestral land. My father, who was five years of age at the time of his return to Goa with his mother, proudly recalls in a memoir published many years later: "Our house in Goa was one of the largest and best in the village. Goans abroad made it a point of honor to build the best house they could afford in their village. Goa was sprinkled with uninhabited houses or ones whose sole occupant was often an aged mother or aunt of the owner.........there was no question of getting rent for them. Rather, you had to pay people to live in them. Goa was then living largely on earnings of her sons abroad, driven to leave Goa for lack of opportunities at home. My father and uncle followed the general example; and my grandmother, their mother, lived in that house, all alone till she died."

In this ancestral village of Moira, my father attended a Portuguese primary school, of which he says: "People imagine that all or most Goans know Portuguese. Very few do. I myself acquired none. The only Portuguese I can remember being taught was to read Portuguese words, each word longer than the one before, without the slightest inkling of their meaning. ... But Konkanim, the native language of Goa, I learned from my mother. I have not forgotten the Konkanim I learned then." Two years passed and then, at the tender age of seven, my father was old enough to join his two elder brothers as a boarder at St. Mary's School in Bombay. Not long thereafter, my grandmother departed Goa for a second time to rejoin her husband in British East Africa. Perhaps if my grandparents had not lived apart for an extended period, she might have helped steady my grandfather's hand and rescue him from a downward slide that resulted in the loss of his fortune. We will return to the trajectory of my father's and grandfather's lives in the following chapters, but now it is time to speak of the remarkable little territory called Goa and the unique hybrid community that evolved there and forms a backdrop for our family's story.

Goa's zenith---an era to which the name Goa Dourado, or Golden Goa, has been attached---was attained centuries ago, during the first hundred and fifty years of Portuguese rule. This followed the "discovery" of Goa in 1498 by Vasco da Gama in a continuation of his voyage to India from the coast of East Africa, as mentioned in a previous chapter, and Goa's subsequent invasion in 1510 by soldiers led by the conquistador Alfonso de Albuquerque. From this initial foothold in India, the Portuguese, with rapidity, rapacity, and great religious zeal, established a far-flung eastern maritime trading empire, and Goa, its administrative and ecclesiastical capital, became a rival to Lisbon in wealth and splendor. At the turn of the 15th century, the Muslim city of Goa---Goapuri at that time---was already a center of commerce, whose reach was then greatly extended by Portuguese dominance of the Indian Ocean and the trade routes from Europe to Asia. Goa and Lisbon became "huge warehouses," with hundreds of ships arriving and departing yearly at their harbors. The bazaars of Goa overflowed with goods, individual streets being devoted to pearls from Bahrein, porcelain and silks from China, velvet and lace from Portugal, drugs from the Malay peninsula, spices from southern India. At the same time, the Portuguese were distinguished from other European powers by also bringing great ecclesiastical zeal to their conquest. In addition to market-places and palaces, churches and convents sprung up in a remarkably short period, creating, for their time and place, a city rivaling Lisbon, which some called the *Rome of the East*. The era known as Goa Dourado lasted for a century and a half, until the Portuguese monopoly of the eastern trade routes was broken by the Dutch and other European powers in the mid-1600s. Portugal then turned its attention to its colonies on the African and South American continents, in particular, to Brazil, and thereafter the legendary city of Goa, located on the island between the two main rivers, entered a period of decline, initially slow and then precipitous.

The ruling Portuguese increasingly began to rely on members of the local populace for day-to-day administration and commerce. They were drawn, in particular, from the Christianized upper castes, and some of them, over the course of time, became exceedingly prosperous. Palatial residences were built by these rich Goan families, in the aforementioned provinces of Bardez and Salsette, in particular, from the mid-1700s through the early 1800s---an architecture to which the designation Indo-Portuguese is attached. These developments were coupled with territorial expansion of the colony---the so-called New Conquests---in the late 1700s, around the time of the American Revolution. This was the period when the city of Goa itself was abandoned in favor of the new capital city of Panjim, today's Panaji. Goa's civic buildings fell into ruin, their stones often recycled in the buildings of the new capital, although in keeping with the religious sensibilities of the converted populace, many of the key religious buildings were preserved. The Reverend Denis Louis Cottineau de Kloguen published his famous *History of Goa* in 1831 and he observed the following regarding Goa's illustrious past and its decayed present (italics mine):

"The city of Goa is famed throughout the world: few men are ignorant of its name, its geographical situation, and its title of capital of the Portuguese Asia. The part, which it took in the general transactions of the Portuguese in the East, its triple capture in 1510, the glory and wealth which it acquired soon after, and its decay, since nearly two centuries, are recorded in all the books that treat of those subjects; but its local history, the different sites which it occupied, its extent and population at the different periods of its splendor and decline, the state and number of its principal buildings, the time when they were erected, its diverse institutions and laws, the manners of its inhabitants, the different classes into which they are divided, are all very little known, or have hitherto been erroneously represented. What is still less known is the actual extraordinary state of that famous city, and of the populous and important territories which surround it, to which it gives its name, and of which it is still the nominal capital. ……. visitors confine themselves to [the city of] Goa, which is now rather *a collection of churches and convents in the midst of a desert*, than a real city; or to Panji [today's Panaji], which is a new and small town that has nothing absolutely remarkable in it; they never think of gathering informations concerning the provinces of Salsette and Bardes [Bardez], which are far more populous and flourishing than the island of Goa, and constitute the residence of the most wealthy inhabitants."

As was the case with the ruling country of Portugal, the economy of Goa continued to rely on trade and agriculture, and it failed to keep pace with the changes wrought by the industrial revolution. Following a temporary lull, the downward slide of the colony began anew, leading to mass emigration of Goans to neighboring British India and further afield to East Africa (and beyond) during the latter half of the 19th century. *Portuguese Goa fell into a deep, century-long slumber.* When Indian independence from Britain was achieved in 1947, India sought to reunite Goa with the motherland through negotiation, but Portugal continued to cling stubbornly to its colony. Eventually, following an extended period of activism within India and Goa to free the colony, and with all patience exhausted, Prime Minister Nehru sent Indian troops into Goa in 1961 and the Portuguese were evicted within a two-day period. Goa was released to flower anew. And today it is among India's most prosperous states, albeit one of its smallest, on track to reach a new zenith---a second Goa Dourado.

Of course, Goa's history did not begin with the Portuguese invasion of the 16th century. The Malabar and Konkan coastline of western India, where Goa is located, had long been fabled for its spices, sandalwood, and other exotic goods. Borne on the winds of trade, sailors had visited it from ancient times: emissaries of King Solomon and ancient Sumer, Phoenecians, Greeks and Romans---recall the *Periplus of the Erythrean Sea* that was mentioned in a previous chapter---and, more recently, Arabs and Chinese. The Portuguese were relative latecomers. Long before the conquest by Alfonso de Albuquerque, Goa had been ruled, from near or afar, by a succession of Indian dynasties: Buddhist, Hindu, and Moslem. Its ancient recorded history began in the time of the great Emperor Ashoka as part of the Mauryan Empire of the 3rd century B.C., a period during which the Buddha's message was spread far and wide across the land. In a fanciful vein, the residents of my grandparents' ancestral village of Moira entertain the notion that its name "Moira" is derived as a variant of "Mauryan." As the influence of Buddhism waned, there followed a litany of Hindu dynastic rulers over Goa whose tongue-twisting names are of interest only to a specialist in Indian history. (Satavahanas dating to the 1st century A.D., Chalukyas between the 6th and 8th centuries, Shilaharas from the 9th to the 10th, a particularly significant flowering occurring during the era identified as Kadamba-Yadava, between the 11th-14th centuries when Chandrapur---today's Chandor---was the capital, a center of power that later migrated north-west, across the river known as the Zuari to a site on the southern banks of the Isle of Goa.) This Hindu-dominated era was terminated by Muslim invaders from the north, at a time when the great Mughal dynasties became ascendant over the Indian subcontinent. An extended tussle then developed between these so-called Bahamani Sultans of the Deccan in central India and the southern Hindu kingdom of Vijayanagar, ruled from the magnificent temple city of Hampi. Initially, the latter gained the upper hand, and Goa enjoyed another period of great flourishing during the 15th century. Its harbors provided the embarkation point to Arabia and Zanzibar in the west, Gujarat in the north, Calicut and Cochin and the Konkan coast in the south. Timber, betel nuts, spices, coconuts, pearls, and rice flowed from Goa to these near and distant lands, while Arabian horses were a particularly valued import. Seeking to diminish the subsequent Portuguese era, Indians today like to say that this Vijayanagar period was the *true* Golden Age of Goa.

The Bahamani Sultans did not retreat from Goa for long and they returned in 1470 to regain control. Thereafter, disputes developed within their empire, and Goa came under the sway of a particular faction, the so-called Adil Shahs (of Bijapur). It was during this period that the site known as Goapuri on the *northern* side of the Isle of Goa, began to flourish and grew into a second capitol of the Adil Shah sultanate. Palaces and mosques were built, often with material taken from the capitol sites of earlier dynasties to the south that had been superseded. Markets thrived, and an Islamic city took shape. This was the city that Vasco da Gama "discovered" at the end 15th century. (To the Portuguese, the earlier Hindu capitol of Govapuri on the south of the island was called Goa Velha, or Goa of Old. Goapuri to its north was known, more simply, as Goa, and later, as it decayed and was abandoned, this legendary city became Velha Goa, or Old Goa. It is small wonder that these names are themselves often interchanged and confused in the popular literature.) The pre-Portuguese era is summarized in a *Goan* activist's pamphlet entitled *Goa: Goan Point of View* as follows:

> "Before the arrival of the Portuguese, Goa was a Great Emporium of the Orient, a center of international trade and commerce---the reason for the Portuguese conquerors to establish themselves in Goa. Perhaps the commercial prosperity was the reason for the development of a flourishing center of Hindu and Moslem culture. Chandrapura, the present village of Chandor, was chosen by Chandraditya for the capital of his kingdom, a powerful dynasty of South India. Under Muslim rulers, Goa became a meeting place for all Muslims in Southern India,

and a starting point for their pilgrimages to Mecca. Yusuf Adil Shah, Sultan of Bijapur, spent most of his time in Goa and wanted to make Goa the capital of his empire in the Deccan."

Adil Shah's reign over the Isle of Goa and its city of Goapuri was short lived. Highly burdensome taxes had been imposed on the Hindu subjects---indeed, the name Mandovi, the river that defined the northern boundary of the Isle of Goa, is said to be derived from the Arabic "mand" for tax and "ob" for water---and wealthy Hindu land owners in Goa chose to make a pact with the devil: they invited in the Portuguese newcomers to throw out the Muslim rulers. The Portuguese were happy to oblige and, the city being lightly defended, Alfonso de Albuquerque was able to take Goapuri without much of a struggle. However, a few months later, the Sultan of Bijapur returned with sixty thousand troops and succeeded in driving out the Portuguese. But not for long! Albuquerque recaptured the city and, the traditional hatred of the Arabic Moors by the people of the Iberian Peninsula reasserting itself, a dreadful massacre ensued. This massacre of great brutality is detailed in the following extract from a letter sent by Alfonso de Albuquerque to his King in Portugal:

> "In the capture of Goa and the squandering of its farms and the entry into the Fort, Our Lord helped us much, for he wished that we should perform so great a deed and in a better manner than we could ask for. …… I then burnt the city and put everything to the sword, and for days continuously our people shed blood in them whenever they caught and found, no life was spared to any Mussulman and their mosques were filled up and set on fire …… we calculated 6,000 souls to have been killed, Mussulmans, men and women and their militia archers many died; it was, my lord, a very great deed, well fought and well finished ….. this shall be heard all over, and through fear and

astonishment will come great things to your obedience without conquering and subjecting; these shall do no wickedness, knowing that they shall pay for it with great price. …. I leave no tomb or building of the Mussulmans standing; those who are now taken alive, I order to be roasted. A renegade was taken and I ordered him to be burnt."

It should thus have come as no surprise to the Hindu subjects of Adil Shah that the Portuguese were not content simply to oust the Muslims and then depart as expected. Instead they elected to stay and take Adil Shah's place, both literally and figuratively. And thus began a fresh cycle in Goa's long history, a new and truly remarkable hybridization of east and west, to which the name Goa Dourado, or Golden Goa, has become attached.

The Portuguese retained the original Islamic pattern of the city. There were no grand boulevards, rather circles and squares, and a thriving river front that provided the main thoroughfare. Palaces were adapted and recreated, mosques were demolished to make way for churches, and splendid residential villas spread out along the Mandovi river. The former palace of Adil Shah known as the Sabaio provided the initial abode of the Portuguese viceroys ("Sabaio" is an alternative name for Shah). Close by on the waterfront, Goa's ancient fortress was restored and rebuilt according to the new conquerors' needs, and this so-called Palacio da Fortalez dos Vice-Reis---the Viceroy's Palace of the Fortress---later became the viceroy's official residence. Also on the waterfront were located the Armory and the Hospital, and on a hill behind them stood one of the earliest religious structures in Goa---the Church of our Lady of the Rosary. Built in the 1510s and little visited today, it conveys better than any other surviving structure the fortress-like quality of the early religious and the civic buildings that comprised the nucleus of the emerging city. This original architecture is nicely characterized in the book of Helder Carita, *Palaces of Goa*, as being inspired by the Portuguese fortress of the 16th century, "steeped in the vocabulary of power," its aesthetic being functionality rather than decoration and designed to convey "calm, solid, and imposing strength." Close by and predating this church stood Goa's first chapel, dedicated to St. Catherine and one of the key religious buildings of the city. Its origins are described, somewhat dramatically, by Heta Pandit in her book *In and Around Old Goa* as follows:

> "This is the exact spot where the Adil Shahs fell to the Portuguese led by Alfonso de Albuquerque on November 25, 1510 after a ten-month siege. The Adil Shah's city gates were demolished and a simple thatched chapel was erected here by a grateful captain [Albuquerque] and crew. It was natural for Goa's new rulers to declare the saint on whose feast day they won a battle, the patron(ess) of the new city."

This chapel has evolved, over the centuries, into a little architectural gem that stands to the present day. Between it and the aforementioned Sabaio Palace was the See Cathedral, the most important church in Goa, the first structure being built around 1528 and the church elevated to the status of a cathedral in 1534.

If you wish today to get some sense of this emerging city, think perhaps of old Vienna, within the perimeter called the Ring, where once stood the old city walls before they were demolished at the end of the 19th century. A broad river-canal, the so-called Donau Canal, which connects to the river Danube, borders what is today known as Vienna's First District, and the medieval city's dimensions were very roughly the same as those of ancient Goa: about a mile and a half in the direction paralleling the Donau Canal, and three-fourths of a mile in the perpendicular direction. However, my own personal and *visceral* sense of Goa Dourado came not from an extended sojourn in Vienna (during the mid-1980s) but rather during a visit to Portugal itself, to a town called Coimbra about 100 kilometers north of Lisbon. Here is located a revered university, sometimes called the Oxford of Portugal, and one of the oldest in Europe. (It was founded in 1290, beginning its existence in Lisbon and, during the next two hundred years, oscillating between Lisbon and Coimbra.) In 1537, during the reign of Joao III, or John the Third in English translation, and coincident with the rise of Goa Dourado, the university was finally given a permanent home in Coimbra's Alcacova Palace. Built atop a hill, this palace endures to the present day, constituting the ancient but still living heart of the university. Bordered by more modern buildings on all sides, it is reachable by a steep climb along streets that wind upwards from the town of Coimbra. One enters the palace through a once-fortified gate that then opens into a large, austere interior courtyard, and, when I walked around this deserted square, I was overcome by a feeling of deep familiarity, as though some ancient, ancestral memory had been awakened in me. Lingering for what may have been close to an hour, time seemed to stand still, past and future fused into a calm, present moment. Where does such memory reside, whereby birds have the knowledge they need to build their nests? The spider to spin its web? A human being to walk in the footsteps of all who have gone before? Years later, when I compared a photograph of the façade of the Alcacova Palace that was taken within the courtyard and a photograph of the building known as the Archiepiscopal Palace in Old Goa, of which we will have more to say below, I was struck by the astonishing resemblance between the two palaces, each dating back to the time of Goa Dourado.

What of the way of life of the inhabitants of the ancient city of Goa? Alfonso de Albuquerque had been tolerant of *Hindu* religious practices---after all it was the rich Hindu landowners that had issued the initial invitation to him to invade the city---and indeed he even encouraged intermarriage between his Portuguese followers and the locals.

The first three decades of Portuguese rule were marked by hedonistic excess as the newcomers enjoyed the plentiful fruits and newfound freedoms of their conquest. This seems to be typical of the early stages of any colonization and, in a subsequent chapter of our story, we will see a similar excess in the behavior of the early English settlers in Kenya, at a much later period of time. In Goa, a particularly notorious individual was the early viceroy, Dom Duarte de Menezes (1521-1524), who had a fondness for "bad women" and "the theft of public funds," and who was eventually arrested and sent back to Portugal in chains. In the aforementioned *History of Goa*, one finds a short synopsis of every Portuguese viceroy save this particular one, of whom one finds the exceedingly curious entry "Duarte de Menezes I. Governor, id .... id." Cottineau summarizes this initial period as follows:

> "All the ancient travelers expatriate, with what justice it is not easy to ascertain, on the corruption of manners of the inhabitants of Goa, on the profligacy and jealousy of the men, the no less immorality of the women, the frequency of murders, &c. It is certain that the authors of the life of St. Francis Xavier themselves, though Portuguese, give a dreadful account of the state of morals in Goa, at the arrival of that celebrated missionary, who, however in a little time, operated a thorough change for the better, ..."

Enough was enough! Joao III, the reigning monarch in Portugal at that time, sent in his religious marines, the Jesuits, led by the aforementioned Francis Xavier, a kill-joy or a savior depending upon your point of view. He arrived in the year 1542, shortly after the founding of the Jesuit Order itself by the Spanish priest St. Ignatius of Loyola and its recognition by Rome. Saint Francis Xavier, one of the founder's first disciples, should not to be confused with the other equally celebrated Saint Francis of Assisi, founder of the Franciscan Order, and possessed of a nature so gentle that birds were said to alight on his outstretched hands and wild beasts to gather peacefully around him. Paradoxically, members of his Order had arrived in Goa much earlier, accompanying Albuquerque in his not-so-gentle conquest in 1510. The Jesuits belonged to a much more militant order, often called the soldiers of Christ, and with their appearance in Goa the period of religious tolerance came to an end. A year prior to the arrival of St. Francis Xavier, laws had already been passed *ordering the destruction of Hindu temples on the Isle of Goa and banning Hindu rituals,* and soon afterwards, Francis Xavier requested that an Inquisition be installed in Goa. The aforementioned Sabaio Palace was its headquarters and henceforth became known as the Palace of the Inquisition.

Like flocks of migrating birds, adherents of other Roman Catholic Orders began to alight in Goa: the Dominicans in 1548, Augustinians in 1572, and Carmelites in 1612. Each established churches, run by male priests, along with convents for the female adherents of the order. These religious orders were much older than the Jesuits, having each been officially recognized in Europe during the 13th century. Compared to them, the Jesuits were johnny-come-latelys! But what Jesuits lacked in pedigree they more than made up in religious zeal and organizing energy. They were the scholars and the architects of the colony. They founded the first western-style university in the Orient in 1557---St. Paul's College---and also introduced the first printing press to Goa. Showing an appreciation of local culture, they even embarked on the study of the local language, Konkani. But, above all, the Jesuits spearheaded the drive to convert the Indian populace to Catholicism, initially on the Isle of Goa, but soon also in a larger area that came under Portuguese sway, the provinces of Salsette to the south of the Isle and Bardez to the north, which were both formally ceded to the Portuguese by Adil Shah in the mid-1500s. This territory, consisting of the Isle of Goa, Salsette, and Bardez, was apportioned by the Portuguese rulers between the different religious orders, thereby avoiding religious friction by giving each an exclusive zone of activity. Salsette fell to the Jesuits and it was during the period 1560-1613, following the transfer from Adil Shah, that Salsette's Hindu temples were destroyed. Here is a remarkable extract from Cottineau's *History of Goa* that is highly revealing when one reads between the lines. Cottineau, being an ordained Catholic priest, was inclined to defend the church against the charge that fire and sword were the primary means of conversion of the Salsette inhabitants, and thus his is a sanitized and exceedingly charitable interpretation of the Inquisition-backed procedure for Christianizing the southern province:

> "The Jesuits converted a great part of them by the usual and most laudable means; but in order, as they thought, the better to detach the remainder of the inhabitants from the worship of idols, they destroyed the temples and pagodas. This however had a contrary effect; and the Pagans, exasperated at this circumstance, rose up in arms, murdered five Jesuits, and several Portuguese. The Governor then felt himself obliged to use arms likewise to reduce the rebels; and of course did not afterwards permit the temples to be rebuilt."

The northern province of Bardez, on the other hand, was proselytized by the Franciscans, who used less forceful methods than the Jesuits. Nevertheless the main Hindu temple in Moira, our family's ancestral village in Bardez, appears to have been demolished, around 1573. The residents of Moira saw the writing on the wall and very wisely *self-converted* not long afterwards. The following extract from a Moira pamphlet of Teotonio de Souza describes this conversion:

> "There were already some Christians in Moira from 1602 ... I am inclined to believe that they were Portuguese settlers, possibly even married to some native women. There is definitely a reference in the

written Government records to a Portuguese, named Gil Vas Lobo, who owned land that had belonged to the Hindu temple .... Could he have been some Portuguese soldier or official who contributed to the demolition of the Moira temples?

The mass conversion of Moira in the village itself was a unique event in those times when general baptisms were not unusual but were held in the Jesuit college of St. Paul's in Old Goa [as mentioned above] or at the Franciscan College of Reis Magos [in Bardez]. We shall come to the mass conversion of the Moidekars shortly. It took place in 1619, but the account of it as recorded in detail by Fr. Paulo de Trinidade in his *Conquista Espiritual do Oriente (1636)* does not tell us what the real motive for the conversion may have been. In good spiritual, or rather pious fashion of the times, he informs us that *they accepted Christian faith without any other motive except moved by divine grace.* To our more critical and less pious mind such an understanding appears to be too simplistic. The Moidekars had already been experiencing dissensions in the functioning of the village community as a result of some of its [members of the village's agrarian community] having already accepted the new faith for the reasons best known to them. Some serious polarization and internal social contradictions must have already set in. It was clear also that the Portuguese and Christianity had come to stay and would continue encroaching upon the traditional set-up. The wisdom of the Moidekars could foresee the problems and preferred to take the bold step which would preempt further socio-economic contradictions from surfacing."

In much the same way, the entire populace of the Isle, Salsette, and Bardez was converted to Portuguese Catholicism, peaceably when possible, but otherwise by force. This also coincided with a period of extensive religious building in Goa Dourado. The magnificent See Cathedral that stands to this day was constructed over the course of several decades beginning in the mid-1500s. The Archbishop's palace, which was built in the earlier, more severe architectural style, was also initiated during this period and it too survives and has been extensively restored during the present time. During the period 1594-1605, which coincided with the end of the reign of the great Mogul Emperor Akbar in northern India (his grandson later built the Taj Mahal), the Jesuit Order constructed their own great church, the currently extant Basilica of Bom Jesus. It is said that Jesuits participated in the religious and philosophical disputations for which the court of Akbar was famous and that the Mogul Emperor sent craftsmen to facilitate the building of the Bom Jesus Basilica in Goa. Several other churches, which were constructed in the ornate Baroque style of the early 17th century, have also been preserved, in particular, the church named for Saint Cajetan, which was said to be a miniature version of the great Basilica of Saint Peter in Rome, and they helped reinforce the designation of Goa of that time as the Rome of the East. This is not the place to describe these churches of Goa Dourado in any detail, but an excellent account can be found in the aforementioned Heta Pandit's *In and Around Old Goa*.

What will be much more fascinating for the reader is the sumptuous way of life of the Portuguese rulers of the colony. The half-century extending from 1575-1625 is described as the climax of prosperity for Goa Dourado. Ostentatious luxury was the byword, and titles, retinues, and rituals abounded, as is captured in first-hand accounts of writer-voyagers, for example, the Dutch traveler Jan Huygens van Linschoten in *Histoire de la Navigation et de son Voyage es Indes Orientales*, (Amsterdam, 1610):

"The Portuguese, both half-breeds and Christians [the former were the product of intermarriage encouraged by Albuquerque and it is interesting to observe the religious distinction made by this author], keep their families richly and magnificently. They are very respectfully served by their servants, commoners as well as nobles. They feigned a majestic and poised bearing, to be all the more esteemed, and each has at least one servant who carries a veil or cape to protect him from rain or sunshine, another who carries the sword of his master so that it does not hinder the poised smoothness of his gait".

And again, from Francois Pyrard de Laval in *Travels to the East Indies* (Paris, 1615, vol. II):

"These ladies [arriving at church] are helped by at least one man, because they cannot walk unaided owing to the height of their clogs, often half a foot high and not well attached to their feet … then each goes to her place, forty or fifty steps away, which takes her at least a quarter of an hour in getting to, because she walks so sedately and ceremoniously, holding in her hand a string of gold, pearls and precious stones."

Such was the tenor of the time, and upon which Helder Carita in *Palaces of Goa* reflects as follows:

"From domestic etiquette to the protocol for great ceremonies, Portuguese life in India obeyed complex rituals. The newcomers wanted to rival the strict customs of Hindu princes and nobles in both luxury and formality. …….. the most insignificant outing of the viceroy or archbishop – the number of people accompanying him, his right of precedence and the magnificence of his cortege – had no comparison with the practices in Europe. ….. at church, the arrival or departure of a highly-ranked lady required a ceremony that could last quite some time …… . These customs, which were often the subject of amused, if not sarcastic, descriptions of writer-voyagers, were merely

Portuguese attempts to impose some social representation compatible with Eastern ways and protocols. In fact, the etiquette and practices of the Indian kingdoms' own princes and ambassadors had become very similar to those of the Portuguese community. The taste for pomp, the number of pages and armed soldiers, even the use of litters and parasols, used also by the Portuguese, were all evidence of mutual influences and gentle rivalries."

It was mid-way through this high-water mark of Golden Goa---the period between 1575 and 1625 characterized by mass religious conversion and splendid excess---that the Dutch made their first attempt, in 1604, to blockade the harbor of Goa. This was unsuccessful. But eventually, in the year 1643, the Dutch did succeed, although they did not invade Goa itself. This date, near the middle of the 17th century, serves as a marker for the end of Goa Dourado, which Cotinneau describes as a time when the "decline of Goa became so sensible." The Dutch, and later the British, had begun to displace the Portuguese across the Indian Ocean and in East Asia. Portuguese trade routes and various settlements around the Indian Ocean and in the Orient were taken over, ending Portuguese dominance in the East. The Portuguese retained their holdings in Mozambique and Angola in Africa and began to turn their attention from Goa to these colonies and to their vast territory of Brazil in South America.

Now began a phase of transition and transformation in Goa, which has been called its Indo-Portuguese period. As the Portuguese colonists were beginning to withdraw from Goa and move elsewhere, the Portuguese authorities began the process of absorbing and co-opting the local population, in particular, the converted upper-caste Brahmins and Chaddos (second in the caste hierarchy), into the governance of Goa, but simultaneously steps were taken to maintain and secure Portugal's administrative grip on the colony. Thus, for example, the Konkani language of the local inhabitants was officially banned in 1684. There continued to be marked developments within the city of Goa, for example, the presently-extant Church of St. Francis of Assisi dates to 1661, although there is some debate about its time of initiation, because prior structures at this site, which were also dedicated to the saint, had been demolished to make way for the new church. And the famous mausoleum within the Jesuits' Basilica of Bom Jesus, where the body of St. Francis Xavier to this day lies entombed in a magnificent casket, also dates to the end of the 17th century. This tomb was created by the Italian artist Francesco Ramponi, who was sent to execute it by one of the Medici Dukes of Tuscany, Cosimo III, in exchange, it is said, for a sacred relic of the saint, his pillow. Ramponi's experience of Goa is described in his own words as follows:

> "That which filled me with admiration was the sight, every eight or ten days, of the arrival of fleets of twenty or thirty boats: one with a load of linen, another with raw or spun cotton, a third with pepper, a fourth with large quantities of drugs; these goods were being loaded and unloaded and dispersed some to one part of India, some to another,"

and Heta Pandit, in her aforementioned book, states that Ramponi marveled at the "porcelain, furniture, brocades, gold cloth, and silks that came to the Goa markets with Chinese merchants." Although the zenith had long passed, the initial decline of Goa during the latter half of the 17th century was slow and uneven.

From the middle of this century onwards, the ruling Portuguese began to emigrate away from Goa, gradually abandoning their magnificent villas along the Mandovi river. Periodic outbreaks of plague and other pestilence, which occurred within Goa as they did in all medieval cities, also caused dislocation within the city and its environs.

By the early 1700s, the decay was evident for all to see. Visitors wrote of the city itself as having declined from a large and opulent metropolis to little more than the chief town of a very miserable territory. But, simultaneously, the winds of change were blowing across the western world and larger historical forces were at work, resulting in a renewed flowering within the Goan provinces of Salsette and Bardez and an extension of the boundaries of the colony itself. The British, having been ousted from North America in 1776 after the American Revolution, were turning their full attention to India, and they had begun to gain dominance over that subcontinent. Because the other local contestants, in particular, the Hindu and Moslem rulers who opposed the British and who controlled the territory around Goa, had been considerably weakened by this struggle, the British success opened the way for Portugal to expand its Indian colony. These so-called New Conquests were made around 1760, and they resulted in the colony's land area roughly tripling in size. Goa began to assume its current dimensions. This also happens to reflect the current $1/3^{rd}$ Catholic and $2/3^{rd}$ Hindu division of the population, because by that time the Portuguese lacked their earlier zeal for conversion of a newly subjugated populace. It was also around this very date that the Jesuits came into conflict with the King of Portugal and his Prime Minister and were expelled from Goa and other Portuguese territories. Their great Basilica of Bom Jesus was given to the Italian's Order of St. Vincent de Paul, and the two Jesuit colleges within the city of Goa---St. Paul's College and the College of the Rock---thereafter fell into ruin. Not long afterwards, in what seemed like a mandate of heaven, one of the two front towers of the great See Cathedral was struck by lightning and fell down, a disaster that occurred in 1776, the year that was made ever-memorable by the start of the American Revolution. This fallen steeple was never re-built, and, instead, it then became the fashion to design churches with a single front tower.

As mentioned previously, we now begin to see the rapid advance of the local upper caste converted Catholics who were favored by the Portuguese authorities and were increasingly inducted into the administrative and commercial offices of the colony. The successful ones built palatial villas in Salsette and Bardez for which Goa is today famous, their construction dating from between roughly the mid-1700s to the early 1800s, and they are nicely documented by Helder Carita, and coupled with beautiful and illustrative photography of Nicholas Sapiela, in a book entitled *Palaces of Goa*. This Indo-Portuguese period, from the mid-18th to the early 19th centuries, was like a *echo* of the earlier Goa Dourado. During that previous era, as we have seen, the Portuguese had adopted the trappings and rituals of the Hindu and Moslem rulers elsewhere in India. Now, in a curious reversal, the prosperous Catholic Brahmins and Chaddos began to take on the Portuguese trappings of status and power, with titles and coats of arms being bestowed on them by the King, to better induct them into the Portuguese social order. But, simultaneously, these cultural hybrids retained their traditional Indian caste-based social structure, which was reinforced by marriage customs that strongly discouraged inter-caste or inter-racial unions. In particular, they preferred physical accommodations that were suited to their social structures and thus they had no desire to take over the villas of the earlier Portuguese rulers along the Mandovi, which thereafter fell into ruin, along with the other civic buildings of Goa Dourado. The Palace of the Viceroy was abandoned at the beginning of the 1800s. A few years later, in 1812, the Inquisition was shuttered and its palace headquarters allowed to fall into ruin. In 1835, the Augustinians were ousted from Goa and a similar fate befell their huge religious complex within the city. In time, the Dominican Church and the Carmelite Convent on the hill behind it also disappeared. Stones from these structures in the old city were undoubtedly used to build new structures closer to the ocean, just as they had transitioned in the past from the ancient capital of Govapuri to the city of Goapuri. The official declaration of the new capital of Panjim came in 1843, barely a dozen years after the publication of Cotinneau's history. All that remained in the old city were some religious buildings, and even fewer civic structures, scattered here and there in a wasteland bordered on the north by the Mandovi. *Golden Goa had turned to clay!*

Thereafter came yet another phase in Goa's long history, the mass emigration of Catholic Goans as the colony fell into a deep slumber. The Portuguese had failed to bring to Goa the new mode of industrial production and its accompanying transportation based on the railroad and steam-powered locomotive---a single miserable railway line connected the extensive system in the larger India with the principal city in Goa. The diaspora of Catholic Goans to Karachi, Bombay, and beyond, is documented in a continuation of the foregoing quotation on conversion in the Moira pamphlet of Teotonio De Souza as follows:

> "At the time of the mass conversion of Moira [during the Goa Dourado period] there were altogether 300 new converts, including men, women and children. The figures we have for a century later are 946. This rose to about 1,965 by the middle of the 19th century. It was around then that Moira was caught in the emigration process, initially to the neighboring British India, then to British East Africa, and finally to the Gulf."

There you have, in miniature, the entire process that extends from Goa Dourado across to the current Catholic Goan diaspora that today touches most countries of the globe. It links my family's ancestral conversion to Roman Catholicism, during the late 16th century, all the way across the centuries to the emigration of my paternal grandparents to Kenya at the end of the 19th, and which we have described in detail in a previous chapter. Today, the Catholic Goan diaspora looks to the land of Goa in India in a manner akin to the way that the Jewish diaspora across the globe looks to the State of Israel.

What is the *larger underlying truth,* or message, of Goa and of the *unique Catholic-Goan* community, within and without Goa's boundaries, which has been the focus of attention in the extended historical survey of our present chapter? The answer, as we shall see in the next, is that *it is large, and, at the same time, it is small.*

Chapter 6

CHURCH, CASTE, AND CLUB

When Portuguese rule came to an abrupt end in 1961 and Goa was reunited with the Indian republic, the economy of the former colony was almost medieval. But, by the early 1980s, when I paid my first and only visit to the land of my ancestors, Goa's reincarnation as India's newest state, and its resulting modernization, was already well under way; for example, in 1961 only three out of Goa's approximately 370 villages had electricity, but by 1980 all but a few isolated villages had electric power. Today, at the onset of the 21st century, Goa has undergone a true renaissance, emerging as one of the Indian Union's most attractive and prosperous states, albeit one of its smallest in size and population.

As we have seen in previous chapters, my paternal grandparents---and, as we shall see later, my mother's family also---belonged to a community called Catholic Goans, who, over the course of four and a half centuries of Portuguese colonial rule, had evolved a unique hybrid culture, a blend of Iberian-Latin and Hindu customs, which they then carried with them as they scattered across the lands of the former British and Portuguese Empires. The term International Catholic Goan Community (ICGC) has been used by the social anthropologist Stella Mascarenhas-Keyes for this network of people, now living in significant numbers in far-flung cities such as Bombay, London, Toronto, Lisbon, Nairobi, Bahrain and Sydney. For its defining center, or focal point, the ICGC continues to look to the Indian state of Goa, where Catholic Goans now comprise roughly a third of the current population, predominating nearer the coast and especially in the provinces of Salsette and Bardez; the remaining population of Goa is largely Hindu, with a small smattering of adherents of other faiths. Members of this Roman Catholic community attend *church* every Sunday, yet they continue to be conscious of *caste* status, particularly in matters of marriage. Love marriages frequently occur, but partners are expected to be of the same caste, and social discrimination will ensue if this rule is violated. The Catholic Goan is an intensely social creature and social *clubs* are focal points for the community, providing sporting venues and facilities where the many holidays and other highlights of the Goan calendar are celebrated with dancing of the Latin variety, feasting on the tastiest of fish and meat curries, and much singing and merry-making. The entire community---adults, children, the elderly---comes together to celebrate such events.

Church, Caste, and Club are thus the three defining characteristics of the ICGC. First and foremost is the Roman Catholic religion, the very fulcrum of ICGC identity, which Mascarenhas-Keyes describes as follows:

> "Catholicism played a central role and was the main idiom through which beliefs and actions were articulated. It is important to emphasise the specificity of Catholicism as opposed to the generality of Christianity. LCG [Local Catholic Goans] were converted to one of the most orthodox forms of Christianity which had rigid dogmas,

doctrines, rules and regulations, elaborate ecclesiastical and episcopal structures, and a worldwide network of churches, convents, schools and other institutions to which all Catholics had potential access. Moreover, Catholics were indoctrinated to believe that they were the chosen few, and such exclusivism fostered encapsulation rather than interaction, except of necessity with 'pagans', be they Protestants or non-Christians.

Through Catholicism a number of structural changes occurred in the LCGC [Local Catholic Goan Community]. Portuguese surnames and Christian names replaced Hindu ones; Catholic Canon Law, rather than the law of Manu or other Hindu sages circumscribed the choice of mate; only monogamy was allowed; celibacy became an honourable rather than a despised state as among Hindus; ecclesiastical office [in churches and convents] was open to both celibate men and women, thus providing a recognised role for women outside marriage which did not exist in Hinduism; an ecclesiastical career was eventually open to anyone of any caste unlike in Hinduism where the priesthood was inherited and limited mainly to Brahmins; and finally, burials replaced cremations and a physical after-life by a spiritual one. The religious exclusivism was compounded by a strong territorial patriotism. Although as Catholics they were part of a universal church that transcended geographical boundaries, LCG were at the same time firmly attached to the soil of Goa, their motherland, and birthplace of their ancestors. The strongest attachment was with the ancestral village…… ."

As we have already noted, the initial Portuguese colony of the early 16th Century, which centered on the Isle of Goa between the two rivers, was a hedonistic place and tolerant of local customs. But this ended with the arrival in 1542 of Francis Xavier, subsequently canonized and now Goa's patron saint, who spearheaded the conversion of the local population. After his evangelizing efforts in India, which extended over a period of almost a decade and included the introduction of the Inquisition to Goa, Francis Xavier proceeded to Japan for two years and then, while trying to gain entry to China, he succumbed on December 2, 1552 to a tropical fever on a small island off the Chinese mainland. His body was interred in quicklime, a standard practice designed to hasten its decomposition prior to transport for formal burial elsewhere. According to a report written in May, 1554, which was said to be, in part, an eyewitness account and, in part, based on reliable first- and second-hand information, three and a half months after his burial, the grave was opened and the body of St. Francis Xavier was found to be

> "entire and intact and no part of it decomposed. The body seemed to be of a living man. It had a good and fragrant odour …… all the clothes and the shoes preserved entire. There was no disintegration caused by the lime. Astonished at the novelty of the thing, they brought it to the city of Malacca … ."

In Malacca, the body of Francis Xavier was reburied, but nine months later it was again disinterred, placed in another coffin, and transported to Goa, where it arrived in March, 1554. The report of a Jesuit priest continues:

> "It was being transported in a coffin still containing the lime: fifteen months had elapsed since his death and the body was placed in lime and carried from one place to another. The flesh was still soft and thick. It had not been consumed either by the lime, or by the earth, or by the worms. It gave off a pleasant odour."

In Goa, the body of St. Francis was given over for public viewing and veneration, where it caused a huge outpouring of religious fervor at the so-called *First Exposition*. It was then re-interred in the Church of St. Paul on the Isle of Old Goa, and thereafter the coffin was periodically reopened for public viewing, each such exposition becoming a central event of the Goan religious calendar. In 1698, over a century later, it was placed in a grand mausoleum designed by the famed Italian architect Francesco Ramponi, within the nearby Jesuit-run Basilica of Bom Jesus. Over the course of centuries the body has become progressively mummified, but expositions continue periodically, and practicing Catholic Goans, to this day, accept the legend of its miraculous preservation after death. Doubters on the other hand---taking our cue from the "doubting" Apostle Thomas, should we call them "doubting-Francis-Xavierites"?---claim that it was all an elaborate hoax perpetrated by the Jesuits, through the use of some secret embalming process, in order to give their religious order added status over competing denominations.

Although the Portuguese had very deliberately sought to obliterate the Hindu religious and cultural identity of their colonial subjects in Goa, any reputable social anthropologist will assure you that this objective is almost impossible to achieve. For example, the foregoing legend of the miraculous preservation of the body of St. Francis-Xavier remains entirely consistent with Hindu Yogic tradition, and innumerable other instances where Hindu customs persist come to mind. A particularly amusing instance involves a holy water fountain---a standard feature of every Roman Catholic Church---which once stood at the entrance to a church in our family's ancestral village of Moira, built after the self-conversion of its population. Long afterwards, it was discovered that the pedestal of this fountain had been made from a *Shiva lingam* (a religious symbol abstracted from the penis), which had been recycled from the destroyed Hindu temple in Moira. Myriads of Catholic converts had long been crossing themselves, unknowingly or perhaps even knowingly, in homage to the old God of Destruction, Shiva. I encountered yet another such example when visiting Goa's nearby Calangute beach, famous for its wide expanse of white sand. The sharp angle of the beach makes for a dangerous undertow in the water that can quickly drag an unwitting bather out to sea, and the local Goan fisher folk, I was told, would sometimes refuse to go to the aid of a bather in distress. "It is One for the Sea," they would say, harking back to the days of Hindu human sacrifice. And, of course, every Catholic Goan child is familiar with his or her mother's Hindu-derived ceremony for removing the "deesth," or evil eye, which involves incantations of a Catholic prayer, in conjunction with a prolonged waving of the maternal hand over the child, from head to foot, sometimes accompanied by the sprinkling, even the burning in a stove, of prescribed chilies and spices.

In other ways, however, the conversion of the population of Goa to Roman Catholicism was all too successful. Its centuries-long reinforcement through fear of the Inquisition ensured that the imported Catholic faith did not become hybridized or subsumed by the earlier Hindu religion in a way that one finds, for instance, in the Mayan areas of southern Mexico. In that country, I recall a visit to the Church of San Juan de Chamula, near the town of San Christobal de las Casas in the deep south of the country, where the Mexican Indians had wrapped their ancient Mayan tradition in the outer trappings of Christianity, creating an aura within their church that was markedly different from my experience of the churches of Goa. The latter have retained a Roman Catholic authenticity, their survival having been ensured by the religious zeal of the local adherents of the faith and achieved, over the centuries, through repeated expansion, embellishment, renovation, and restoration of structures that date back to Goa Dourado. To this day, the Goan Catholic priest plays a central role within the ICGC and indeed, until quite recently, the eldest son of a family was often destined for the priesthood. Enforced celibacy of the Catholic priest resulted in the typical Goan family tree having numerous dead ends, a fate that we have seen has also befallen the *non-religious*, civic structures of Goa

Dourado. In contrast to its churches, the only civic building that has survived the ravages of time and disease is the Archbishop's Palace, and that too because it served a religious purpose.

Caste is the second defining feature of the ICGC, whose members continue to observe caste rules of hierarchy and partition derived from their distant Hindu ancestry, albeit in a significantly watered-down manner. If human cultures and subcultures within the Indian subcontinent are compared to animal species then caste can be viewed as the mechanism that ensures their survival. This is the view to which the defenders of the caste system have subscribed. Without caste, they say, India would have the blandness of the United States, blended together like a curry made from too many different spices, leaving only a dull and heavy flavor. Hinduism, thriving as it does on the social multiplicity of the caste system, has given to India the sense of a vast coral reef, they say, where many different forms of living can coexist, each in its own ecological niche: *"India, a magnificent cage of countless compartments,"* in the words of the great Indian philosopher and poet Rabindranath Tagore. But the overarching reality of caste is that it is a mechanism designed to ensure the domination of one group, over another, over yet another, ..., within India. The preservation of an unfair power structure, this is the root of the caste system. To my mind, it is the scourge of modern India, reinforced by an instinct even more corrosive than the human drive for power, which Patrick French has captured exceedingly well in *India: A Portrait* (italics mine):

> "Casteism remains one of the aspects of India life that is hardest to understand. It is unlike other forms of prejudice, where antipathy is linked to envy or desire: an anti-Semite will ask why "they" do so well in business and a white racist will fear and envy apparent black physical prowess. Prejudice against outcastes is built on the idea that you will be *polluted* if you go near them. They exist only to serve, and

then at some distance. *It is a uniquely powerful form of social control, since it is total and self-replicating.* The higher castes can only remain high if they have others to look down upon. So in the not too distant past, a boy would brush against an elderly sweeper in a corridor and his mother might whisper to him: "Don't touch, you will get a scale or turn into an insect!" A prayer or purification might follow. This would lodge in the child's memory, and even as he grew older and less traditional---or even international, living in Europe or America---*the instinctive response, the flinch, remained.*"

French's conclusions are made within a description of one of the oft-forgotten, founding fathers of the Indian Republic, the highly accomplished Dr. Ambedkar, who played a significant role in formulating the Indian Constitution and who happened to be of the Dalit caste, also called Untouchables, and he notes the following:

"In the 1930s he [Ambedkar] announced that Hinduism was beyond reform, and shortly before his death in 1956 [many years after Indian independence in 1947] converted to Buddhism along with his second wife, Savita, and many thousands of his followers."

But in Goa it was different! Following the Portuguese conquest and the conversion of the local populace, the hard edges within the practice of caste amongst Catholic Goans began to erode and undergo an evolution. Albuquerque, the Portuguese conquistador of Old Goa, had encouraged intermarriage from the outset. Portuguese women being in short supply, this generally meant a marriage between a Portuguese male and a Goan female, and since women are the primary transmitters of culture within a family, the children of mixed-blood would generally assume both a Roman-Catholic and a caste identity. Among the larger populace that converted to Catholicism, but continued to marry within their own race, caste identity would naturally endure, even as its practices became ameliorated by the new religious teachings. By the time of Cottineau's *History of Goa*, which was published in 1831 and of which we have spoken at length in the previous chapter, the author was able to make the following very insightful observations that are worth quoting at length (italics mine):

"Although the Indians of Goa, in embracing Christianity, have not retained, like those of the Jesuit and Pondicherry Missions [in other parts of India], all those distinctions of castes and ancient usages of Paganism [Hinduism], which have been considered indifferent to religion [presumably Roman-Catholicism], they nevertheless keep up that distinction only in respect to marriages, which are most generally, though not always, contracted between members of the same castes; *these castes may therefore be now considered as the different tribes into which the ancient Israelites were divided.*

The first class or caste is that of the Europeans, or their children, born in the country, without the probable intention of remaining in it. This class is very small, and confined to the Viceroy, or Governor, and some of his Subalterns, as well as some officers of the army, a few seamen, the Archbishop, and a very few clergy men and monks, and lastly a few soldiers, who marry in the country, and whose children are immediately numbered in the second or mixed class.

The second class is that called the *mistiss,* or mixed class, very much similar to that called among the English, Indo-Britons [nowadays Anglo-Indians], though it has a more extensive comprehension, than that term; for it includes even natives of pure European blood, but established in the country since the first generation. .... Because, as they say, *"If there is no mixture of blood, there is a mixture of air;"* these families, all very respectable, are not numerous. After these, come all those who are of mixed European and Indian blood, and who are much more numerous and the greater part poor. The second class, however, is still the smallest after the pure Europeans; those descended only from European parents though after several generations, differ very little in complexion from the Portuguese of Europe; the others have a lighter or deeper shade, according to the proportion of Indian blood they have in them.

The third class, or caste, is that of the *Brahmins*; they are held in high esteem and consideration, though excluded from the greatest privileges of the Europeans and their descendants, ………. The Brahmins are the less numerous Indian caste, but much more numerous, indeed, than the two preceding put together.

The fourth class or caste is that of the *Chados,* who, ….. pretend to be of the *Chatria,* or royal or military caste, (though many authors maintain that that caste, as well as that of the *Vaisias* [the merchant caste of Hinduism], is now extinct.) This caste, in the colony of Goa, is more numerous than that of the Brahmins, and held in equal estimation, though inferior with respect to rank.

The fifth class is that of the *Soodras* or *Sudras,* which, as in other parts of India, forms by far the greatest part of the population. In this colony, the Sudras are more numerous than all the other Christian inhabitants, both of the superior and inferior castes. They are not so much respected as the Brahmins or Chados; *they formerly were not admitted even to hold orders, but that and all other privileges of the two superior tribes, are now conceded to them,* though they are not by far held in the same estimation.

The sixth class is that of the inferior Sudras, who follow the profession of fishermen and other viler occupations, ……, and likewise the outcastes. They are similar to the *Parias* in the southern provinces of India, or the coolies and other low castes in the north. *They are, however, not treated with the same contempt as among the heathens* [Hindus]*;* but they must remain in their own professions, and are not admitted to any place of trust whatsoever, which are held not only by the higher, but ordinary servants, who are all of the superior castes; though reduced by poverty to serve, in order to gain their livelihood.

The *slaves* of Mosambique [Africans] may be considered as the last Christian caste. They are employed like the preceding."

And now Cottineau summarizes the behavior of the castes within the Catholic Goan community as follows (italics again mine):

"The members of the five superior tribes, very rarely marry out of their castes, except the soldiers and some few Europeans of distinction, who may, but very rarely, enter into bonds of matrimony with some descendants of pure European blood. It sometimes, however, happens that men of one caste takes wives from the inferior ones, and the children of such cases retain the caste of their father; but never will a man of a superior caste give his daughter in marriage to a man of an inferior one; and generally such mixed marriages take place between a man and a woman of the caste immediately following that of the man in inferiority. *Except in regard to marriages, the five superior castes agree in most things; they make not the slightest difficulty of eating together, and of concurring in all the other circumstances of civil life; they likewise make no distinction of food whatsoever.*"

Catholic Goans had thus found a way to sideline the scourge of caste to a considerable extent and Hindu India today has much to learn from their experience. This great amelioration of caste and the opportunity to collectively share food and drink made possible the third facet of the Catholic-Goan identity to which we have alluded above, namely, the *Goan Club*. This is a gathering place for the community to celebrate key holidays of the social and religious calendar, and, in between holiday celebrations, a place to relax after the day's work is done or after church attendance is completed on a Sunday. The social club is an important feature of British life imported to its colonies, and the ICGC, especially in East Africa, patterned their clubs on the British model, whilst simultaneously giving them a unique character derived from Goan adherence to village-based social life. Since Goa has always been a mecca for good dining, let us take the opportunity here to briefly describe Goan food itself, less complex than much of southern Indian, but leavened by Portuguese and Arabic influences that have yielded a delightful, hybrid cuisine. Here are recipes for two dishes, one non-vegetarian and the other vegetarian that capture its essence. Recipes for these dishes, called Sorpotel and Maraguay, or Feijoada, respectively, can become extremely elaborate and the following are *highly simplified* versions that require very few ingredients and relatively little cooking time:

Ingredients for Sorpotel:
1 kilogram belly pork (if unavailable, substitute any fatty pork)
½ kilogram pork liver (if unavailable, substitute beef liver)
2 level teaspoons cayenne (red) pepper
1 level teaspoon turmeric (yellow) powder
1 level teaspoon salt
1 large onion

In a large pot, boil the pork and liver in 2 cups of water, replenishing water as needed. Remove meat and preserve the juice in the pot. Cut up the two meats separately into small pieces, say ½ inch or less. In a frying pan, fry the fatty pork and remove to a platter. Similarly, fry the liver in the rendered pork fat and remove to the same platter. Dice and fry the onion till brown. To the large pot, add the pork, liver, onion, spices, and salt. Cook for about ½ an hour. Ideally, if you can wait, keep the dish in the fridge for a day or two, warming it each day. By the third day the flavors will have blended to perfection.

And here is the vegetarian recipe based on red kidney beans (called maraguay in Swahili), again reduced to its essence:

Ingredients for Maraguay:
    1 cup dried red kidney beans (do *not* use canned beans)
    1 large onion
    3 or 4 medium-sized potatoes
    ¾ level teaspoon cayenne (red) pepper
    ½ level teaspoon turmeric (yellow) powder
    ½ level teaspoon salt

Wash and drain the kidney beans. In a large pot, boil them in plenty of water, on medium to medium-high heat, until the beans are soft but retain their shape. Do not use a lid to avoid boil-over and replenish the water as necessary to keep the beans covered. When the beans are ready, add the spices to the pot. Slice the onion and add to the pot. Peel the potatoes, cut into 1 inch pieces and add to pot. Turn heat to very low, put on lid, and simmer for 20 mins to ½ hour. The potatoes should have softened but still retain their shape, shedding enough to thicken the gravy and make it rich. Serve with a large spoonful of mayonnaise and warm chapattis or tortillas.

Over time, by fine tuning the ingredients, in particular the quantity of the spices and the cooking procedure, you can make these dishes your very own. And, if desired, much more elaborate versions of both recipes can be found in Gilda Mendonsa's *The Best of Goan Cooking*.

    In dreams and in real life, humans often symbolize themselves by their houses, and if one desires a *metaphor* that encapsulates the essential character, or identity, of the Catholic Goan, which we have considered in some detail above, then one can find it within the pages of a delightful book, *Palaces of Goa: Models and Types of Indo-Portuguese Civil Architecture* by Helda Carita (with accompanying photography by Nicolas Sapieha). Here are given descriptions and photographs of a variety of palace-like villas belonging to prominent Goan families, now mostly in a state of disrepair and faded splendor. The entertainment areas---the reception room, the ballroom for Latin-type dancing, the common dining hall---face outwards towards the world, while within lie the rooms for daily living and the chapel for religious worship, a "cage of many compartments," often placed around a secluded courtyard on the Hindu pattern. *Portuguese on the outside and Indian on the inside* is our sought-after metaphor.

And if, on the other hand, one seeks instead an *analogue* for 16th century Goa Dourado itself, where our entire story began, i.e., a more recent hybridization of people, culture, and religion, then one can find it by advancing forward in time by three centuries to the 19th century island of Zanzibar on the other side of the Indian Ocean, a mirror image of sorts for the little province of Goa. Cut off from the African mainland by a short stretch of water, akin to Goa's separation from the rest of India by the mountain range of the Western Ghats, with complementary wet and dry seasons tied to the monsoon winds, Zanzibar, too, had a Golden Age, which was built on dominating the world's supply of cloves and the abominable trade in East African slaves. *Its history, too, is writ large and yet simultaneously is also small.* In Zanzibar, and along the nearby coast, the conquering Arabs had converted the local populace to the Muslim faith and freely intermarried with them, creating the hybrid Swahili people and their now widely-used language. Oman on the Arabian Peninsula (as discussed in a previous chapter) and Portugal on the Iberian Peninsula were roughly comparable in scope and importance when they developed their colonial outreach centered on Zanzibar and Goa, respectively, and these two countries were the conveyers of the cultural and religious influences of Islam and Christianity, respectively, to their distant colonies. After Great Britain ended the Arab domination of the East African coast and, in particular, the slave trade, Zanzibar quickly began to wilt on the vine, just as Goa Dourado had begun to fade when the Dutch ended the Portuguese domination of the eastern commercial trade routes. Of course one should not carry the analogy too far, because Goa Dourado, in its heyday the product of a newly-awakening Europe during the time of the Renaissance, was much more splendid than Zanzibar, and because the hinterlands, of which each of the two colonial creations was still a part and which their colonized inhabitants continued to carry within their bones, were very different in their nature. In the case of Goa, the hinterland was the vast, rich culture and civilization of the Indian subcontinent. In the case of Zanzibar, Eastern Africa provided a vastness and richness of a different kind: open spaces, boundless reaches of sky, a stunning scenery, the soaring, abounding sense of freedom of an untamed continent. Over the course of the 19th and 20th centuries, while memory of the golden ages of Goa and Zanzibar faded into oblivion, the East African nations of Kenya, Uganda, and Tanganyika came into existence, and, on the other side of the Indian Ocean, the diverse states of the Indian subcontinent became melded into a single nation, both of these singular developments occurring under British colonial rule. India won her independence from Britain in 1947 and the African nations a decade and a half later. And today, at the outset of the 21st century, Zanzibar finds its identity as part of the African Republic of Tanzania---a name composed from Tanganyika and Zanzibar---while Goa prospers in lockstep with the Indian Union.

Social Club and Social Caste, Sacrifice of the Body and Blood of Jesus Christ, Sacrifice to the Dark Depths of the Sea! A nimble fellow is the Catholic-Goan. Like a trapeze artist, he has walked a tight-rope that divides two very different cultures: Latin and Hindu. But now, following the ouster of the Portuguese in 1961 after a rule of four and a half centuries, Goa is already well advanced into the process of returning more fully to her Indian roots. The beliefs, practices, and values of the great shaping force of Hinduism, which had for centuries only acted in an indirect way, creating a psychological rift that separated the Catholic-Goan community from traditional India, are reasserting themselves, and Catholic-Goans today are busy redefining their identity anew.

To the mouth of the Mandovi River, near the city of Panaji (Panjim), flat-bottomed barges carry a rich load of iron ore destined for export to distant lands. The seas yield a bountiful harvest of fish; the land a bountiful crop of rice, coconuts, cashews, and spices. Goa, at one time the Jewel of the Kings of Southern India, subsequently a rival to Lisbon for wealth and splendor, has mineral resources, fishing, agriculture, and above all, the transforming face of tourism. This today is a land with a past *and* a future!

Chapter 7

MACKIE WILL MAKE MY NAME

We now pick up the thread of our story from the time of my grandmother's temporary return in 1913 with her children to Goa, the Portuguese enclave described in detail in the last two chapters, from whence my grandparents had emigrated to Kenya at the turn of the 20th century. Following their two-year sojourn in Goa, my father was old enough to enter St. Mary's, the Jesuit-run boarding school in Bombay where his two elder brothers were already enrolled, and, not long afterwards, my grandmother rejoined her husband in East Africa. But for my father the passage to the Indian subcontinent marked an entirely different turn of events. Apart from two or three short holidays in Kenya, he was not to return to the land of his birth for another twenty-one years.

St. Mary's School where he was enrolled was founded in 1864 in a section of Bombay---today's Mumbai---that was considered fashionable at the time. It was run by the Jesuit Fathers, who, as we have already seen, had first set foot on the Indian subcontinent in Goa during the mid-16th century. Goa had provided the stepping stone for expansion to other parts of India and when the Jesuits ran afoul of the King of Portugal two centuries later and were expelled from Goa and other Portuguese dominions, the Society of Jesus was already well established in British-India. Its highly rigid Catholic orthodoxy---Jesuits are sometimes called the Marines of the Catholic Church---was counterbalanced by a devotion to education and scholarship, and, in pursuit of these objectives, the Jesuits continued to establish missions, schools, and colleges in other parts of the Indian subcontinent.

St. Mary's purpose was to educate the children of the administrators of the British Empire in India and the school thus catered primarily to boys of European descent. However, English-speaking Indians of a westernized patina, for example, Parsees and Goans, were also admitted, albeit in smaller numbers. The school comprised both a boarding school and a day school, with boarders living in the school's hostel and day scholars living at home with their parents or guardians. The boarding school was itself partitioned horizontally, so that boys of similar age were grouped together, an organization very unlike the vertical partitioning within the British public school system with its attendant problem of "fagging," a form of bullying where younger boys are required to perform servile tasks for older ones in their "house." For dining purposes within the boarding school at St. Mary's, there was yet another division into First Class and Second Class sections. One got slightly better fare as a boarder in the First Class, and a form of reverse discrimination was imposed on non-European boarders who were only admitted into this First Class category. Education at St. Mary's was far from inexpensive. But my grandfather was well-off at that time and could easily afford the boarding and school fees for his three enrolled sons.

Being torn from the bosom of his family at such a tender age must have been emotionally difficult for my father, although he was not entirely on his own, because his two elder brothers, my Uncles Vincent and Eddie, were also enrolled at St. Mary's. Initially, my father and his brothers were placed in the boarding school, but after my grandfather lost his fortune, they were reduced to day attendance and housed with a relative in Bombay. Day boys and boarders attended classes together and no distinction was made between them so far as education was concerned. But in my father's time there was an unusual *vertical* partition in the school based on racial lines: the European Teaching Division "A" catered to Europeans, Anglo-Indians (boys of mixed European and Indian parentage), and Eurasians (typically from other parts of Europe), and the English Teaching Division "B" was for the others. My father recalls that the quality of the teachers and the syllabus did not differ and racial prejudice of this sort had very little adverse effect because it issued more out of the policies of the British rulers than any practice or desire of the Jesuit Order.

The British had created a very remarkable educational system based on a prescribed syllabus and a tiered sequence of examinations administered by the University of Cambridge in England that operated uniformly across the empire. Boys who failed the examinations were winnowed out so that school classes, or *standards* as they were called in the two teaching divisions, progressively diminished in size and eventually were merged, and, in my father's case, this occurred when he was around the age of fifteen. Thereafter scholastically he always took the first or second place in the merged higher standards and thus, in his own words, no "inferiority complex" grew from the earlier racial partition. However, Goan boys tended to be looked down upon by the boys of European descent and Goan boarders sometimes hid their origins. A boy with the easily identified Goan name of "Fernandes" might change it to "Ferns" in much the same way that in the United States, Marcus Rothkowicz became Mark Rothko---the renowned artist---in order to obscure his Russian-Jewish origins. But the three Nazareths at St. Mary's remained proudly and openly Goans and their surname remained unchanged. My father's eldest brother, Vincent, in spite of the prejudice against Goans, became in effect the head boy of the school, and was entrusted with the keys of the dormitory and study hall, not to mention the "tuck-shop" where snacks were sold. Indeed, my father recalls only a single adverse effect on him arising from prejudice---an incident highly revealing of his character---that followed his success in the Junior Cambridge Examination in Standard VII. In his words: "I had topped the class and had apparently done well enough to merit a scholarship, provided I could claim some European ancestry. The Principal appeared anxious that I should stake a claim and seemed ready to accept me at my word. But that I could not bring myself to do. So I did not get the scholarship."

My grandfather's financial situation having turned dire, the two elder brothers returned to Kenya after their school years. But my father's brilliance led him on to St. Xavier's College, another Jesuit-run institution in Bombay, which was founded in 1869 only a few years after the founding of St. Mary's, and which took its name from the great saint of the Jesuit Order of whom we have spoken earlier. (St. Xavier's recently made its way into the American media when President Barack Obama, during a State visit to India, held one of his town-hall, question-and-answer meetings with Indian students at the college.) Remittances from my grandfather in Nairobi were small, rare and uncertain and life for my father was "one long anxiety". During his first two years he resided with his grand-uncle, who lived in a small flat about five minutes walk from the college, where living conditions were austere. My father and two other boarders slept on the floor, laying down their bedding each night and rolling it up in the morning, and he recalls surviving on a diet consisting primarily of hard-boiled eggs. However, his fortunes changed for the better during his second two years through the kindness of a Jesuit mentor, Father Fell, who found him a place rent-free in the college hostel, on condition that he served daily at Mass. It was also during this time, perhaps during the long periods he spent on his knees before the altar, exchanging incomprehensible incantations in Latin with the presiding priest, that he began to question the tenets of the Roman Catholic religion. Eventually, over the course of several years, he "lost his faith," as they say in Catholic parlance, which I view as yet further evidence of his individualism and freedom in thought, although the writings of Bertrand Russell also helped to sway him in his turn to agnosticism. However, my father never lost his "deep respect and affection for the dedicated men of the Catholic priesthood and especially for the Jesuit Fathers" in whose schools he was educated. (And, indeed, it was this high regard that led him to decisions that had a profound effect on my own future---but that is left for a future telling!)

By the remarkably early age of twelve, my father had determined that he would become a lawyer and he appears never to have wavered from that goal. Perhaps it had something to do with the injustice his father had suffered at the hands of creditors in the loss of his fortune, or perhaps it was simply a strong inbred sense of justice itself. During his college years, he worked single-mindedly and extremely hard towards his objective, leading him to achieve first place in his B.A. examinations at St. Xavier's College and the award of a Gold Medal, but also very nearly to a nervous breakdown. The good Father Fell again came to his rescue by providing a free holiday in Khandala, a resort town south of Bombay, in the mountains known as the Western Ghats. It was during his time at St. Xavier's that my father also got his first taste for politics through involvement in student affairs. But, given the need to earn money to pay his college fees by winning scholarships, his studies always came first and foremost. My mother, who despite my parents' differences was ever proud of my father's accomplishments, was fond of saying of this early baptism of fire: "Your father would not be the man that he is today if his own father had not lost his money."

My father graduated from St. Xavier's College in 1930, the same year that his father, my grandfather Joachim Antonio Nazareth, passed away in Kenya, hopefully peaceful in the knowledge that his son Mackie was indeed well on his way to "making his name." Following graduation, my father had begun attending classes at the Government Law School with the intention of qualifying as a lawyer in Bombay. But then came one of those accidents of fate that place one on a completely different path. Some time earlier, during a short visit to Kenya, he had met Thome Emar De Souza, the son of one of the most prominent merchants in Nairobi, a contemporary of my grandfather, who had remained prosperous even as my own grandfather's family had fallen back into poverty. Thome Emar had befriended my father and generously offered to help him if he needed money to complete his studies, and had readily responded when, upon returning to Bombay, my father had applied for small sums. Shortly into his law studies, my father had written to his new friend to ask whether it would be possible to practice law in Kenya after he qualified in Bombay. In his subsequent memoir, my father describes what ensued: "He mistakenly (it was for me a fortunate mistake) informed me that I had to qualify in Britain. So I asked him if he would loan me the money. He had agreed---without interest and without security---most generously." It was indeed an extraordinarily generous act of friendship and trust!

And that is how my father emerged four years later, during the depths of the world-wide Depression, a trained barrister from the Inns of Court in London, and saddled with a debt of thirty thousand Kenya Shillings, an enormous sum in those days. Despite initial loneliness, he had soon settled into a regime of intense study during those years, and, in a chapter in his memoir titled "Student-At-Law," he describes this period of growth and experience. Writing in some detail of his successes and failures, he recalls, in particular, his winning of the Special Prize of the Council of Legal Education in Criminal Law and Procedure and simultaneously the Poland Prize of the Inner Temple (one of the Inns of Court) as follows:

"I must linger a while on this great day in my life. The evening of the day the [law] examination results appeared in *The Times* I came down to dinner as usual. Suddenly the Warden [of his hostel] rose in his place and proposed a toast to me. Everybody rose. Being toasted was for me a novel experience. I too rose. And from beside me came a loud whisper; 'Sit down, you bloody fool.' Bloody fool or not, this was a glorious, immortal moment, for the competition was an Empire-wide competition and the prize is often not awarded on the ground that there has been no student of sufficient merit to warrant an award. It gave me greatly-needed, or at least greatly-valued, self-confidence. Greatly needed, particularly in Kenya, where I was, in another three years, to enter an atmosphere where race was all, and individual merit in people of non-European races was little or nothing."

Later upon graduation at the Inner Temple---called to the Bar as it is termed in England---he was awarded yet another prize (called the Profumo Prize in Common Law), one of the stipulations attached to it being that he was required to read in "Chambers" for a year, English legal parlance for a type of apprenticeship to a senior lawyer so as to better learn the tools of the trade. Once again, Thome Emar generously agreed to finance him for a fourth year. In his memoir, my father describes in some detail his training and his contributions as an apprentice, recalling that it was tremendously worthwhile and that "it helped very greatly to give me a balanced judgment and at the same time self-confidence in my practice and generally in my opinions."

In June 1934, his time as an apprentice in Chambers came to an end, and, after a short holiday en route in Paris and Switzerland, he boarded a ship in Naples, Italy, bound for Kenya, eager to rejoin his brothers and sisters at long last, and ready to embark upon his professional life as a lawyer in Nairobi. His four years in Great Britain had been, in his own words, "a warm, enriching, satisfying and fruitful experience."

Chapter 8

KENYAN PIONEERS

By the time of my father's return to Kenya in 1934, the pioneering phase of the British protectorate turned colony was already well in the past. Today, perhaps its most widely identifiable representative is the Baroness Karen von Blixen, known to the larger world by her writer's name, Isak Dinesen. She had arrived in Kenya in 1914---just a year after my father had left with his mother for India as a child---accompanying her husband, the Baron von Blixen, from whom she derived her title. (They were divorced in the early 1920s.) Together, they created a coffee farm, in an area that today is an upscale suburb of Nairobi named "Karen" in her honor, and from this pioneering adventure grew her memoir, *Out of Africa*, which would establish her reputation as a writer and project Kenya forever into the imagination of her readers across the globe. No one has better captured the magic of Kenya's essence as she does in the opening, and indeed the very best, passages of her book, and only a deep love and attachment to the land and the way of life born of it can create writing such as this:

"I had a farm in Africa, at the foot of the Ngong hills. The Equator runs across these highlands, a hundred miles to the North, and the farm lay at an altitude of over six thousand feet. In the day-time you felt that you had got high up, near to the sun, but the early mornings were limpid and restful, and the nights were cold.

The geographical position and the height of the land combined to create a landscape that had not its like in all the world. There was no fat on it and no luxuriance anywhere, it was Africa distilled up through six thousand feet, like the strong and refined essence of a continent. The colours were dry and burnt, like the colours in pottery. The trees had a light delicate foliage, the structure of which was different from that of the trees in Europe; it did not grow in bows or cupolas, but in horizontal layers, and the formation gave to the tall solitary trees a likeness to the palms, or a heroic and romantic air like fullrigged ships with their sails clewed up, and to the edge of a wood a strange appearance as if the whole wood was faintly vibrating. Upon the grass of the great plains the crooked bare old thorn-trees were scattered, and the grass was spiced like thyme and bog-myrtle; in some places the scent was so strong, that it smarted in the nostrils. All the flowers that you found on the plains, or upon the creepers and liana in the native forest, were diminutive like flowers of the downs,---only just in the beginning of the long rains a number of big, massive heavy-scented lilies sprung out on the plains. The views were immensely wide. Everything that you saw made for greatness and freedom, and unequalled nobility.

The chief feature of the landscape, and of your life in it, was the air. Looking back on a sojourn in the African highlands, you are struck by your feeling of having lived for a time up in the air. The sky was rarely more than pale blue or violet, with a profusion of mighty, weightless, ever-changing clouds towering up and sailing on it, but it has a blue vigour in it, and at a short distance it painted the ranges of the hills and the woods a fresh deep blue. In the middle of the day the air was alive over the land, like a flame burning; it scintillated, waved and shone like running water, mirrored and doubled all objects, and created great Fata Morgana. Up in this high air you breathed easily, drawing in a vital assurance and lightness of heart. In the highlands you woke up in the morning and thought: Here I am, here I ought to be."

To people in the United States, Karen Blixen and her lover Denys Finch-Hatton are better known as the fictionalized characters played by Meryl Streep and Robert Redford in the filmed version of *Out of Africa*. Finch-Hatton himself was a handsome and erudite rogue, Eton and Oxford-educated, and one of the earliest aviators in Kenya, who had simultaneously flown in and out of romantic engagements with a variety of women. He eventually met the fate common to such adventurers, crashing his Gipsy Moth aircraft when out on an elephant-scouting flight near today's Tsavo National Park, and he was buried at a site overlooking the Rift Valley, close to the Blixen farm. Not long after his death, following a collapse of commodity prices during the Great Depression, Karen Blixen's operation went bankrupt and in 1931 she left Kenya to return for good to Denmark, her country of origin. Her departure came just three years before my father embarked on his own journey in the opposite direction, returning to make a home in the land of his birth after a twenty-one year absence. There was *no intersection* between their two experiences of early Kenya.

Another creature of romance during that period was the almost-as-famous Beryl Markham, who had also shared her bed with Denys Finch-Hatton (and many others, including two members of the British royal family). In 1906, at the tender age of four, her father brought her to Kenya where he too had established a farm, at a place called Njoro, located about a hundred miles north-west of Nairobi, near the railway line to the great inland lake. There Beryl Markham grew up wild, a native child, her playmates the children of the Nandi Murani, a warrior tribe of Hamitic enhnicity akin to the Masai. She recalls her early days in her memoir *West with the Night* as follows:

> "Nor has my memory of the farm at Njoro ever left me. I would stand in the little yard before the first of our few huts, and the deep Mau forest would be behind me at my shoulder, and the Rongai Valley would be sloping downward from the tips of my toes. On clear days I could touch, almost, the high, charred rim of the Menegai Crater and see, by shading my eyes, the crown of [Mount] Kenya studded in ice. I could see the peak of Sattima behind the Liakipia Escarpment that got purple when the sun rose, and smell the cedar wood and fresh-cut mahogo and hear the crack of the Dutchmen's whips over the heads of their oxen."

And the remainder of her paragraph is so poetic in its description that it is best set to verse and read like a stanza that might have been written by Dylan Thomas:

> "Sometimes the syces [farm laborers] would sing at their work,
> And all day long in their pastures
> The mares and foals would romp and feed
> Make the soothing sounds that horses make with their nostrils
> Their hooves rustling the deep grass bedding in the stables.
> At a little distance their imperious lords, the stallions,
> Fretted amiably in more luxurious boxes
> And grew sleek and steel-muscled
> Under the constant care."

As a young adult, Beryl Markham became a breeder and trainer of race horses, and later Kenya's first female aviator, flying her monoplane across the skies of East Africa and delivering mail and passengers to the remotest parts of the country. It was only the premonition of a fellow-aviator and friend, Tom Black, that had kept her from being aboard the fatal flight when her one-time lover Denys Finch-Hatton, who had introduced her to aviation, met his untimely end. In September 1936, Beryl Markham gained world-wide fame as the first person to fly solo across the north Atlantic from *east to west*, a flight that prompted the title of her memoir, which was first published in 1942 following her third marriage, to the writer and journalist, Raoul Schumacher. The authorship of this book is a matter of controversy. Her biographer, Errol Trzebinski, whom we have encountered in a previous chapter, maintains that *West with the Night* was jointly written by Beryl Markham and her husband, and that much of the early manuscript was in his handwriting. But this misses the point---the book itself is clearly based on her remarkable life, and the poetry and freshness that marks every line must derive from her telling, and more importantly, her living of it. The book was initially a best-seller, but later slipped into obscurity for a period of several decades, until its discovery and re-publication in 1983 by a small press in Berkeley, California. Today, one can hold her memoir in one's hands once more and be captured by the magic of her writing and of a life that seems to have been a long, continuous adventure, and marked by a series of surreal coincidences. One can hardly begin to recount them here, but a particularly striking one involved a fellow-pilot who had disappeared on a cross-country flight and was given up for lost. Returning from a delivery mission, Markham had by sheer chance spotted sunlight reflected from the wing of a downed aircraft, far out in the bush land, and, through pluck and skill, had managed to land her aircraft on a bit of flat ground nearby. In her own words:

> "Circling again, I saw that in spite of a few pig-holes and scattered rocks, a landing would be possible. About thirty yards from the

Klemm [the lost pilot's downed aircraft] there was a natural clearing blanketed by short, tawny grass. From the air I judged the length of the space to be roughly a hundred and fifty yards---not really long enough for a plane without brakes, but long enough with such head wind as there was to check her glide.

I throttled down, allowing just enough revs to prevent the ship from stalling at the slow speed required to land in so small a space. Flattening out and swinging the tail from side to side in order to get what limited vision I could at the ground below and directly ahead, I few in gently and brought the Avian [her aircraft] to earth in a surprisingly smooth run."

The lost pilot was barely alive and she revived him with water. But no sooner had she got him aboard her aircraft to bring him back to Nairobi for medical care than who should appear over the horizon, in a little billow of dust, and lit up by the light of the setting sun? None other than a certain Indian Sikh, Bishon Singh, a one-time worker on her father's farm, who had rescued her as a child from a surprise attack by a full-grown lion that a fellow farmer kept as a "pet." She had not set eyes on Bishon Singh for a decade or more, and yet there he was, out of the blue and in the middle of nowhere, at the head of a little caravan of three donkeys---each donkey fully loaded with supplies and attended by a Kikuyu "boy" as African male servants were insultingly called in those days---travelling cross-country to re-provision a little shop that he now owned somewhere far out within Masailand. Markham's description of this utterly surreal and by no means atypical experience covers more than a few pages and it must be read in its entirety in the original before one passes judgment on its verity.

British Kenya during the nineteen-twenties and thirties was also notorious for the hedonistic lifestyle of the "Happy Valley" crowd, settlers mainly of English origin, who had made their homes in the so-called white highlands, in a valley adjacent to the Aberdare mountain range and not far from the colonial town of Nyeri, located in the foothills of Mount Kenya. Alcohol, drugs, and sex were the life blood of these aristocrats and adventurers, with wives and husbands being swapped, and every carnal appetite catered to. In Nairobi, their headquarters was the Muthaiga Country Club, which was equally infamous for their carryings-on. But the term "Happy Valley" itself is identified more with an attitude rather than with any particular geographic location such as Nyeri or Muthaiga. The interested reader, aided by a Google search using the keywords 'Happy Valley Kenya', will find numerous pointers, in particular, to a Wikipedia article that tells the full story, and another useful source is Juliet Barnes' recent book *The Ghosts of Happy Valley*. In many ways, "Happy Valley" is reminiscent of the lifestyle of the Portuguese colonists in Goa at its inception, of which we have spoken in a previous chapter. Indeed, it is perhaps typical of the early days of any colonial conquest.

What of the immigrants of Indian (Asian) origin in Kenya? For them it was a very different story---they lived in an alternate, *parallel universe*. As we have already seen, Indians played a key role in the construction of the railroad from the coast to the great inland lake, but after its completion in 1901, the majority of the thirty thousand imported Indian labourers, mostly from the Punjab, returned to India. Thus, at the turn of the twentieth century, the population of Kenya was comprised of approximately five *hundred* whites (people of European origin), seven *thousand* Asians (people of Indian or Arabian origin who had chosen to remain on in Kenya), and three *million* native Africans. The completed railway facilitated the arrival of a fresh wave of European and Indian settlers along its inland route, and the immigrant population of Kenya grew accordingly. By 1921, there were ten thousand whites and twenty-five thousand Asians resident in the colony, again vastly outnumbered by the native peoples.

The great historian Alexis de Tocqueville has characterized immigrants to the North American continent as having "a mania for commerce," and much the same could be said of the Indians of East Africa. As we have seen in earlier chapters, this mania had been pursued, across the Indian Ocean, for millennia. To their eternal shame, Indians had financed the centuries-old Arab-led slave caravans that penetrated the interior. More recently, they helped in the organization of the caravans of the 19th century explorers, they introduced "begaree" to East Africa, a form of porterage used in India to transport goods from village to village, and, after murram roads like that named for Sclater were constructed across the East African colonies, Indians introduced "kalami," a type of four-wheel Indian cart that was pushed by as many as ten porters and was capable of carrying a load of fifteen-hundred pounds. Thus it was quite natural for Indian immigrants to very quickly adopt and take advantage of the new mode of transport made possible by the arrival of the automobile. Like the railroad, its introduction to Kenya at the beginning of the 20th century was tinged with romance. It is recorded that the very first automobile to be unloaded from a steamship at Mombasa in December 1903 was the exotically-named *De Dion-Bouton*. Because there were no petrol (gas) stations in those days, it carried its own supply, and, the condition of the roads being terrible, automobiles like it had to be transported up-country to Nairobi by rail. Indeed the first automobile journey from Mombasa to Nairobi was only completed two decades later, in the early 1920s, by an equally exotic and hyphenated adventurer, Douglas Galton-Fenzi, driving an automobile identified as a *Riley 12/50*.

The road situation gradually improved within the urban areas. In Nairobi, shorts strips of tarmac came into existence around 1922 and spread to other towns by 1930. Beryl Markham describes these roads in the vicinity of Nairobi (which had dictated her choice of a career in aviation) as follows (italics ours):

"I had been working out of Nairobi as a free-lance pilot with the [aforementioned] Muthiaga Country Club as my headquarters. Even in nineteen-thirty-five it wasn't easy to get a plane in East Africa and *it was almost impossible to get very far across the country without one.* There were roads, of course, leading in a dozen directions out of Nairobi. They started out boldly enough, but grew narrow and rough after a few miles and dwindled into the rock-studded hills, or lost themselves in a morass of red muram mud or black cotton soil, in the flat country and the valleys. On a map they look sturdy and incapable of deceit, but to have ventured from Nairobi south towards Machakos or Magadi in anything less formidable than a moderately powered John Deere tractor was optimistic to the point of whimsy, and the road to the Anglo-Egyptian Sudan, north and west through Naivasha, called 'practicable' in the dry season, had, when I last used it after a mild rain, an adhesive quality equal to that of the most prized black treacle."

Her description, in turn, lends color to the following delightful passage from J.S. Mangat's *A History of the Asians in East Africa c. 1886 to 1945*, which captures the spirit of pioneering Indians nicely and is about as good a summary of the entire Indian enterprise in East Africa as I have found anywhere (italics again mine):

"The introduction of motor transport in the mid-1920s by the otherwise much-maligned Indian country trader is particularly significant, for it opened up areas which he had previously penetrated by carts and wagons to more speedy economic development. As Sir Edward Griff [a colonial administrator] later commented: 'I have been deeply struck by the enterprise and spirit and the disregard of risk with which Indians in many places make themselves the pioneers of road transport...' and referred to the Indian lorry driver *'whom I have frequently seen without lights, without brakes, apparently without tyres, and with an engine which looked like conking out at any moment, pushing trade through the most inaccessible places...'.* In fact, in their various capacities as fundis [carpenters] and dukawallas [shopkeepers], cotton ginners and building contractors, wholesalers and retailers, lorry drivers and clerks, and indeed in every conceivable business activity, the Indians played a crucial role in the overall economic development of the East African territories."

As for the African tribal people, theirs was a tale of displacement and exploitation. We have already seen the manner of their subjugation in Hobley's graphic description in Chapter 2, and, in the early days of the protectorate, a certain patrician mindset of the administrators prevailed, also typified by Hobley. A passage in his 1929 memoir compares early Britons with native Africans and can again be quoted by way of illustration (italics mine):

"It has occurred to me to visualize mentally the opinions which the Roman invaders of Britain may have formed of the semi-savage inhabitants of Britain in B.C. 54. Julius Caesar and his captains were men who, for that period, were in the front rank of world civilization. They were imbued with literary traditions, for it was the age of giants, Cicero and the like. They were steeped in Greek culture as well as their own. They were representative of a nation of great achievements, and they and their forebears had built up a mighty state analogous in some ways to our own Empire. What would they have thought of the skin-clad Britons; with what contempt would they have compared their own elaborate Pantheism to the weird magical worship of the Druid priests at their sacred oaks! They must have looked down on them as veritable '*wa-shenzi'* (Swahili---savages). Would any Roman have acknowledged that these rude people had in them the makings of a great nation? I doubt it. The four hundred years of the Roman occupation of Britain had a profound effect upon their subjects. Our occupation of the East African hinterland does not yet extend to forty years. *Who can forecast the effect of two hundred years of patient work on the African native?* No analogy is perfect, but the one I have quoted may have some value, and I, for one, would not venture to assert boldly that the African can never be capable of playing a great part in his own government."

It would never have crossed Hobley's otherwise-noble mind that, a mere three and a half decades later, Kenya would be an independent, self-governing nation. His was arguably the prevalent attitude among the British colonists when my father was taken back to India as a child in 1913, a time when the centuries-old human caravan routes, snaking inland from the coast to the shores of the great lakes of the Rift Valley, had barely given way to the smooth railway-line of iron that stretched from Mombasa, via Nairobi, to the largest lake, renamed for Queen Victoria. There were relatively few automobiles on the streets of Nairobi and no airplanes in the skies overhead. Nairobi was a frontier town! But the Kenya to which my father returned to make his home in 1934 at the mature age of twenty-six, during the depths of the world-wide Great Depression and just a few years before the onset of World War II, was a far different country from the one that he had left at the age of five. The Nairobi of dusty streets and a rambling, ramshackle Indian bazaar had turned into a pleasant colonial town, with broad-paved avenues downtown, and leafy, segregated residential suburbs, where the influx of European and Asian (Indian) settlers now lived in the comfort that only a plentiful supply of cheap domestic labor and a delightful climate could make possible. By then, the population of European or Indian origin had roughly doubled once again from the numbers quoted earlier, with the native African population growing more slowly within the range of three or four million. The attitude of the British rulers had changed from the patrician condescension of the early administrators to outright racial discrimination, spearheaded by white settlers, many of whom had come to Kenya via South Africa, and their racist and separatist mindset had become firmly entrenched in the governance of Kenya. Gross inequities of land distribution, a "color-bar" in the townships and the fertile Highland areas, and totally inadequate political representation for the people of African and Asian ethnicity were central characteristics of the colony.

There is no shortage today of works of scholarship on the political or economic history of East Africa that cover these inequities, and these books can be recommended to the interested reader---a few are listed in the bibliography. But, from my own perspective, it is the intrepid travelers and the early administrators of the protectorate, later turned colony, whose first-hand accounts provide the more pertinent observations, capturing the true flavor of the time. One of the most interesting of such travelogues is that of Negley Farson, who has been described as being "in the great tradition of Stanley." (However, recalling the descriptive quotations of Stanley in Chapter 2, I would add that Farson in his writings demonstrates a much greater degree of empathy than does Stanley towards both hunted beast and the oppressed native.) Negley Farson was the grandson of a notorious American Civil War general, James Negley, a commander in General Sherman's army during its march of destruction across the Confederate States following their Civil War defeat. Born in New Jersey in 1890, he was expelled from college, immediately emigrated to England, and thereafter embarked on a career in journalism---a foreign correspondent with a life-long thirst for adventure. He is said to have been "present in Red Square when the Bolshevik Revolution broke out, to have interviewed Ghandi at the time of his arrest during the struggle for Indian independence, witnessed bank-robber John Dillinger's naked body in the morgue just after he had been shot down by Hoover's men, and met Hitler who characterized Farson's small blond son as 'a good Aryan boy'." In his private life, which is described as being equally turbulent, "he partied with F. Scott Fitzerald" and supposedly "out-drank Ernest Hemingway."

It was during the late-1930s, only a few years after my father's return to Kenya, that Negley Farson undertook an adventure across the African continent, a journey that began by ship from Durban in South Africa to Dar-es-salaam, the main port of Tanganyika, where he would rendezvous with his wife who arrived by a different route. (Tanganyika is today's independent nation of Tanzania, the former colony of Germany that had fallen into British hands following the German defeat in World War I.) Acquiring a Ford V-6 in Dar-es-salaam, they embarked together on a journey across East and Central Africa, driving from one coast to the other. The result was an extraordinary travelogue, *Behind God's Back*, published in 1940 just after the Second World War commenced in Europe.

On board ship at the start of his journey, Farson had already begun to reflect on the attitude of the white settlers, some of whom had made their way to Kenya from South Africa, others more directly from Europe:

"It can be taken as an axiom that a white man never intends to do any heavy-duty manual work in Africa. His life's job, as he considers it, is to supervise black labour. He is dependent upon the native for all the connection with urban civilization. Until he is willing to do this work himself, he will never be able to free himself from the black man. The black man must, therefore, be kept under control. The reservoir of black labour must be preserved. More than that, it must be made to work. Left to himself, the native would do only the barest minimum of work, merely enough to keep himself alive, if that. A system, therefore, was long ago invented of taxation to make a native work. Whether it is a head or hut-tax, the result is the same---a large number of natives must be absent from their reserves a certain number of months every year, in order to earn enough money to pay this taxation. And any *surplus* of labour, which the white man feels he may reasonably do without, may be segregated in Reserves---African Whipsnades." [Whipsnade is the name of a famous zoo in England and here used as a metaphor for the Bantustans of South Africa.]

Farson describes the system of inequitable taxation in neighboring British-Tanganyika, the starting point of his African journey, which is representative of the colonial system in general, and which we will paraphrase here rather than quote directly. Up to the outbreak of the Second World War, there was no Income Tax in Tanganyika. About a third of Tanganyika's total revenue came from the Native Poll Tax---"poll" here refers to a head, or population, count and is not being used in the sense of the right to vote---which in 1937 amounted to around 672,050 Pounds, a "pound" being a unit of currency equaling 20 Shillings. The natives paid a poll tax that ranged from four to fifteen shillings, with an equal amount for each extra plural wife. This was graded according to district and the native's earning capacity; and, in some parts of the central province the poll tax of eight shillings a year appropriated about half the native's earnings for that year. On the average, the native paid about 10 per cent of his yearly earnings to the Government. In contrast, the European poll tax in 1937 totaled only 44,000 Pounds. This tax was adjudged as follows: for each non-native adult male earning between Pounds 300 and 400, the tax was Pounds 4 per annum; between Pounds 400 and 500, the tax was Pounds 5 per annum; and so on, up to earnings that exceeded Pounds 700, when the tax increased to Pounds 11 per annum. In other words, *Farson observes that while the native was forced to pay at least 10 percent of his earnings in tax, the white man wasn't paying much over 1 per cent.*

Does this not sound familiar when one recalls the current inequity of the tax system in the United States, where the billionaire Warren Buffet points out, and to his credit has sought to rectify, that his secretary pays much more tax as a percentage of income than he does. It's an age-old story that repeats itself again and again, down through human history. And this perhaps explains why arch-conservatives in the United States falsely distract their audience with the assertion that the first black president of the United States, Barack Obama, in seeking a greater measure of tax fairness in the United States, derives his inspiration from a socialist Kenyan father that he, in fact, hardly knew. They foolishly fail to comprehend, or perhaps knavishly fail to transmit, the larger, underlying lesson that is to be learned from the extraordinary *unfairness* of colonial Kenya. The United States is indeed developing on the pattern of a colony, only this time the "colonizers" are the global corporations and financial barons that dominate our political scene, and whose standard-bearers are to be found primarily within the conservative movement of today's Republican Party, and the "colonized" are the hard-working but often ignorant and easily-misled everyday Americans whose labor is extracted for an appallingly-low minimum wage.

Negley Farson and his wife continued on to Kenya, whose roads Farson describes, echoing Beryl Markham in a foregoing quotation, *as some of the most atrocious he had ever encountered in all his travels.* He observes that the idea of Kenya as a white man's country had firmly taken root in the minds of the European settlers and notes the various economic and political structures put in place to enforce it---the restrictions of land ownership to whites only on some of the best lands for agriculture and ranching (the so-called "White Highlands"), the social color bar coupled with segregated residential areas within the towns, the concentration of all power in the hands of the white settlers---of which we will have much more to say in subsequent chapters. In particular, he describes a visit with politically-moderate British settlers in the Rift Valley, when his hostess had taken him to the vicinity of Nairobi to meet a senior figure in the Kikuyu tribe. When the appointment fell through, he continues as follows (italics mine):

"Instead, I was obliged to spend the day listening to a colonial official. At that time the Kikuyu were upset because the white settlers were forcibly ejecting the 'squatters' from their farms; these were Kikuyu natives who, in return for the permission to live on these lands, gave the white owners a certain amount of free labour in exchange. Some of these Kikuyu had been living on the same land for several generations. It had been accepted, in their simple minds, that they had some claim to it something slightly more than a moral dual ownership. But their cattle had been getting in the way of the settlers' cattle; and so they were told to move. Be evicted, in fact. As the places selected for them were some 30 to 85 miles further from Nairobi, the Kikuyus claimed that this would ruin them; they would not be able to get their stuff to the Nairobi market.

And I now give you verbatim (because from their talk you may know them!) the 'sporty' way this official answered the desperate Kikuyus.

"I said to them, 'Oh, but you blokes must remember this is *our* market---what? We built Nairobi. If we chaps hadn't built Nairobi, what would you blokes have done then---what?' "

Amazing, I know; but this conversation is accurate. I stopped the car and made notes of it as soon as I escaped from him.

....   To all questions on topics like this, this complacent official, he was a 'military fellah', replied: "Oh, those blokes are *agitators*! Mustn't listen to stuff like that. These blokes here (the Kikuyus), they're getting politically-minded, too. No end of trouble. When these natives learn the error of their ways......"

When we turned around to drop down into the Rift Valley again, begin the 100-mile return trip, and forget the futile day in the majestic vistas of Kenya, my hostess was silent for about forty miles. Then she turned to me:

"I know it's bad," she said, "But you must remember one thing: We British are the only race who would feel *worried* about such things. We do not do them with an easy conscience. That's something to be said."

I admitted that it was something, to feel remorse when you have done someone a wrong; *"But you will never forgive the natives,"* I said, *"for having made you do it."*

This quotation captures, better than anything I could say, the attitude of the colonial administration and the white settlers towards the native Africans (and Indians) in the colony to which my father had returned. Twenty-one years had elapsed since he had been sent as a child to be educated in British India. The retention of the vivid memories of childhood usually starts around the age of six or seven, which in my father's case corresponded to the age when he was enrolled as a boarder in St. Mary's School in India. Thereafter, until the completion his studies in Bombay and England in 1934, he hardly ever returned to the land of his birth and thus Africa was never really "in his blood," and neither was Portuguese Goa. Rather it was India itself, and indirectly the colonial power that ruled the subcontinent at the time, which had shaped his emotional being and his political outlook and mindset, and this allegiance to India he makes clear in his memoir, *Brown Man Black Country*, as follows (italics mine):

"I had no narrow tendencies to regard myself as being merely a Goan, and not a part of the Indian community. In England, the Goan in me had receded into the background and the Indian part of me had come to the fore. I could identify myself only as an Indian, for Goa was an unknown, an almost invisible speck in the vast maze of India. *So it had become natural for me to think of myself as Indian and to be proud of it.* India, with all its blots and stains, with much to cure and reform, a subject country then, I yet was proud and devoted to, and I shared the hope that its future would be worthy of its past."

In Kenya, my father embarked on his professional career during the depths of the Great Depression. He served primarily the legal needs of the Indian community and in a short chapter titled "The First Ten Years" of his aforementioned memoir, he recalls this period of his life in the following way:

"I started life in Kenya with a debt of about Shs. 30,000, a very large sum in those days. The value of money then can be gauged from the salaries I paid my staff in 1935 when I started to practice: Shs. 75 per month to my typist, a Goan, and Shs. 125 to the law clerk, a Muslim. I could not start practice at once, much as I wished to. The Rules of Court provided that one could not be enrolled unless one had resided in Kenya for at least six months.

.....

Having commenced practice in January, 1935, I was towards the end of that year joined in partnership by Porus Aderji Mehta. This was one of the finest things that has happened to me. We became not merely partners but warm friends, a friendship that has endured to this day, though our communications are few and far between. Every evening we would walk home until we came to the parting of our ways, a walk of some 20 or 25 minutes from the town. He lived about three minutes away from there and I about five.

Mehta is one of the ablest men I have met. He had had a very distinguished academic career, having graduated with a First Class in

Philosophy from Elphinstone College, Bombay. At the Government Law School, where he took his degree in Law, he had won the Inverarity Gold Medal. He was deeply and widely read, a born debater and had had the distinction of leading the Bombay University Debating Team against the Oxford University Team when it visited Bombay. A gifted speaker, he could hold an audience absorbed and entertained for an hour, with notes on a piece of paper no bigger than the palm of one's hand. He was prepared to speak on either side of the question and did not hesitate to speak at short notice. Among those who know him at Nairobi he is something of a legend. I cannot recall anyone I have heard who was as read or as good a speaker. I had the full measure of his outstanding quality, as we sometimes met in debates on opposite sides, he as a member of the team from the Monday Club and I of the Goan Academic Circle.

During the three years that we were partners we made very little money. To make an early financial success in legal practice in the Indian community backing is essential. Neither of us had any, he being a Parsi, I a Goan. The Parsi community had almost no businessmen and the position of the Goans at that time was hardly better. I feel that we did not make as much as even Shs. 200 each per month. We had the misfortune of commencing practice in the depths of the world depression, and it hit Kenya as hard, or harder, than any other country."

Like attracts like, and so you can already see the extreme promise of my father himself and the stellar future that awaited him in Kenya in these fond recollections of his first legal partner and life-long friend.

As for the personal sphere, my father enjoyed what he describes as "a quiet, a pleasant, and a full life," which was lived primarily within the oasis created by fellow Goan immigrants in Kenya. He was a keen sportsman and played field hockey for a team representing the Goan

Club known locally as the RGI (Railway Goan Institute), which was considered to be one of the two top teams in Kenya. He played tennis every Sunday, contract bridge one evening a week at the Goan Gymkhana, and, for cultural activites, there was the aforementioned Goan Academic Circle and the Goan Music Society. (He had an especially deep love for western classical music.) But although keenly interested in politics, he did not have any active participation in either Goan or Indian politics. Politics simply was not in the forefront of his mind; there were more pressing matters to attend to first. A full ten years passed before his enormous debt was paid off. And then, freed of this burden, his legal career began to flourish and an interest in political involvement began to stir. My father was now a man in need of a wife.

Among traditional Indians, at home or abroad, arranged marriages remain the norm. A family with a daughter or son of marriageable age is ever on the lookout for a suitable match. At first, discreet inquiries will be made to ascertain parity of caste, creed, education, and status in general. A go-between may then be employed to transmit a marriage proposal, photographs will be exchanged, and, if all passes muster, a chaperoned meeting will be arranged. When separated by distance, prospective partners may write to one another, letters that will often bear traces of a collective, familial hand. The pair will meet again, but rarely will they be together alone. And soon the parents will begin to grow restive in the face of a son's or daughter's indecision: "What are your intentions?" they will ask, or, more pointedly, *"What more do you need to know?"*

Consent having been obtained, or perhaps coerced, the matrimonial machinery will be set in motion and begin to hum smoothly. "Boy" and "girl" will soon be pronounced husband and wife in an elaborate marriage ceremony, where often no expense is spared. And the couple will then have been launched on their socially prescribed journey that leads, in turn, to a new cycle of parenthood, child-bearing and rearing; and, once the time comes for the new generation of children to marry, to the benevolent despotism of guiding their childrens' choice of spouses.

Goans of the Roman Catholic faith adhere to this general pattern, but in a more flexible way, allowing considerably more latitude of choice. As mentioned earlier, a Catholic Goan attends Mass in church every Sunday, yet continues to be conscious of Hindu-derived caste status, particularly in matters of marriage. He or she may marry for love, but will encounter social discrimination if the chosen partner is of a lower caste, and many marriages continue to be arranged in the traditional Indian manner, being viewed primarily as a union of two families, not of two individuals. This was the context within which my own parents were married.

An initiating proposal of marriage from my maternal grandparents was transmitted to my father via a go-between, on behalf of their daughter, Maria Monica Isobel. By any measure she was a good catch. She was very good looking, with an upright, regal bearing. She was also well educated, almost always at the top of her class in high school, and afterwards continuing on to college to obtain a bachelor-of-arts degree, followed by a degree in law (LL.B.). In fact, my maternal grandfather was so proud of his daughter's achievements that whenever he wrote to my mother following her marriage, his aerogramme invariably bore the address "Maria Monica Isobel de Freitas e Nazareth, B.A., LL.B.," with a c/o my father following, almost an afterthought. My mother had other talents as well. She was musically trained on the violin and mandolin, and, during her school years, she apparently also excelled on the sports field as a short-distance runner. However, that last accomplishment was not easy for us, her children, to imagine, because for most of her married life my mother's daily apparel was a sari: gracefully gliding forward on the athletics field, perhaps, but definitely not sprinting to a finish line at full tilt!

I know few details of my parents' courtship save that after a short stay in Bombay my father returned to Nairobi, an interval passed during which letters were exchanged, and he then came again to Bombay to be married in 1944. India at that time was still an integral part of the British Empire and World War II between Germany and Great Britain and its Allies was raging in Europe and around the Pacific Ocean, but the countries of East Africa and India were not under attack and life seemed to proceed in a relatively normal way. Porus Mehta, my father's former legal partner and friend, of whom we have spoken in a previous chapter and who had long-since returned to India, raised the toast at the reception and celebration that followed their traditional Goan-Catholic marriage ceremony, which you see recorded in the marriage photograph at the end of this chapter. And soon thereafter, my parents travelled to Kenya to begin their new life, of which we will have more to say in a subsequent chapter. I was born in Nairobi in 1946, two years later, and a year after my birth my parents returned to India—travelling by train from Nairobi to Mombasa and then onward to Bombay by ship--- in order to be present at the momentous event in August, 1947 when India became an independent nation, and, simultaneously, to present my maternal grandparents with their first grandchild. Both my parents had spent their formative years in and were therefore shaped by India, rather than by Africa, and they both retained a very strong attachment to that country, which they have passed on to me, and thus it was very natural for them to want to be present at the celebrations of Indian independence from Great Britain.

At the time of my parents' marriage in 1944 and when I was born in 1946, India and East Africa were still united within the British Empire and, as our passports declared, we three were officially citizens of the United Kingdom and Colonies. A year later all that had changed, at least for the Indian subcontinent. Now, in place of a single nation ruled by Great Britain, there were two independent nations partitioned between

India and Pakistan. My father eloquently records his memory of these events and reflects on them in the following way:

> "I was present for the independence celebration on August 15 at Bombay and was a witness to the wild scenes of ecstasy of the Indian people in Bombay. The tragedy and bloodbath of partition through which India waded to independence was forgotten and in celebrating that unprecedented event the people gave themselves to unrestrained rejoicing. By the time Kenya's independence was attained in 1963, several African countries had attained theirs, including Tanganyika and Uganda. Independence celebrations no longer had that unique flavour that had marked independence celebrations in India. As Britain and other European countries shed their colonial appendages, exchanging expensive power for lucrative influence with all practicable speed, independence celebrations tended to lose the glamour of the first Independence celebrations of all, those of August, 1947.
>
> But against the euphoria through which India was passing I was not unconscious of the ugly other side of the coin: the undercurrent of the partition and its accompanying massacres. In passing through Lahore on my way to or from Kashmir, where I spent a few days, shortly before Independence Day, I could not leave the train to have a look at the city, as that was too dangerous. The massacres had started. Before that I had heard [Lord] Mountbatten, Nehru [the first Prime Minister of independent India] and Jinnah [Prime Minister of Pakistan] announcing on the radio the impending tragedy of partition. [These were three of the main architects of independence.] Mountbatten's, a highly competent and impressive performance; Nehru's voice coming through poorly yet deeply moving, stricken with agony; Jinnah's cold, narrow, hard, pedestrian.
>
> Later ushering in the dawn of independence, Nehru was to make a speech ("long years ago we made a tryst with destiny"), which must

rank with Lincoln's immortal Gettysburg speech, ("four score and seven years ago"), speeches that will illumine the annals of mankind as long as human memory shall endure, and which has helped to place Nehru in my mind alongside Lincoln among the immortals of mankind."

Of course I have no memory of these momentous events. But I have a validating photograph to prove that I was indeed present, which is shown at the end of the chapter. In this photograph of my mother's natal family, which was taken in Bombay at the time of Indian Independence in 1947, you see me standing upright on my maternal grandmother's knee at the tender age of a little more than a year. My mother is seated next to my grandmother and behind her stands my father. Aunty Lucy, the eldest of the siblings, sits next to my grandfather and behind her is the only son of the family, Uncle Lennie. Standing beside my father is Aunty Freda, and next to her is the youngest member of the family, Aunty Yvonne. We will meet and honor them all in much more detail in a companion book, *Up and About in Nairobi and Bombay*. But, for now, we must return to the "historical collage" that is the main focus of the present book, and, in its next chapter, we will set out to explore the complex relationship between India and Great Britain, prior to the Indian independence celebrations of August, 1947, to which, *as the photograph attests, I was unknowingly a witness.*

A PASSAGE TO KENYA

My Parents' Wedding Photograph

JOHN LAWRENCE NAZARETH

A One-Year Old, Unknowing Witness to Indian Independence

Chapter 9

ON INDIAN INDEPENDENCE

Looking back on that momentous day in August 1947 when India gained her independence from Great Britain---the dissolution of a marriage, so to speak, between the two countries---one can fairly ask the question: after a ruling hegemony over the subcontinent of roughly a hundred and fifty years, what enduring legacy did the Englishman leave to India? How did the two countries influence one another's character in an essential way? In seeking my own individual answer, with the benefit of half a century's hindsight, I will attempt to look at the larger picture on hand, at the palimpsest that was and is India, and beyond the tyranny, pettiness, and greed of the *individual* ruling British officials, which is so well known to anyone familiar with the colonial period.

The first English settlement in India, a small trading post on the site of modern Madras (recently changed to Chennai), was granted by the Hindu rulers of the south in 1639. In such small beginnings is an empire born. Extending control by degrees, the British eventually triumphed in the four-way struggle for control of the Indian subcontinent.

The other protagonists in this struggle were the Indianized Muslim rulers of the north, whose series of incursions, beginning in the twelfth century A.D., culminated in control over most of northern India during the reign of the great emperor Akbar; the Maharatas, who originated from Maharashtra in Western India, and were finally crushed by the British in 1818; and the French, whose fortunes in India were intimately linked with those of Napoleon in Europe, and whose last vestiges of influence are now apparent only in places like Pondicherry in southern India. The memorable year 1776, when the North Americans finally shook themselves free of the British, is also the year when the people of India had begun to almost completely lose their freedom *to* the British. The long shoreline of the subcontinent, coupled with the supremacy of the English navy, and, in particular its control over the sea routes, gave the British a great advantage in the fight for India. A tiny faraway island had forged an instrument that made vulnerable every nation bordering on an ocean. It is difficult today to comprehend the magnitude and extent of control that the English navy made possible. But imagine, if you will, a modern nation of the present century, with economic strength coupled with intelligence, ruthlessness, guile, and energy. Suppose such a nation achieved a mastery of space comparable to the British mastery of the seas, and acquired a *fourth* military wing superior to that of any other country, namely, a space force---the next logical and inevitable step in the progression: army, navy, and airforce. Would not every country in the world be suddenly vulnerable to such a nation?

The subcontinent of India has roughly the same land area, population, linguistic variety, and national diversity as the continent of Europe with Russia excluded. Fragmented into numerous states during most of its history, the Indian subcontinent was united under a common ruler only at rare intervals, most notably, under the Emperors Ashoka (264 – 228 BC) and Akbar the Great (1542-1605 AD). India derives her distinctive quality, her color, so to speak, from Hinduism, just as Europe derives distinctive color from Christianity in all its various denominations---Catholic, Protestant, and Orthodox. Prior to the British era, the Indianized followers of Mohammed held control over much of India. An important consequence of British rule was to drive Islam to the far reaches of the subcontinent---namely to what is now Pakistan and Bangladesh, though, of course, India still has a very sizeable Moslem minority---and to restore India to Hinduism in a secular guise, once the British era came to an end in August, 1947. Furthermore, in the face of the challenge from western ideas during the colonial period, reformist movements sprang up in many parts of India, which sought to purge decadent Hinduism of its dank undergrowths, for instance, dowry, child marriage, and suttee (the practice of immolating a widow on her husband's funeral pyre). Gandhism, assuming both a religious and a political form, is an example of such a movement. So I would say that the first major contribution of the British was to give India back to the Hindus.

Secondly, the British gave this vast land an administrative unity and the infrastructure of a modern state by creating a civil service and a national army. An extensive network of railways was built, but with the aid of Indian capital and labor one must hasten to add. And one cannot underestimate the importance of English being adopted as the lingua franca of a land of fourteen major languages, over five hundred dialects, and at least six major scripts.

Thirdly, India acquired some of the modern means of production during the British period. However, I want to be clear on this point, for I would argue that India modernized *in spite of* British rule rather than as a result of it. Although the industrial revolution first manifested itself in England---recall that James Watt developed his engine in 1775, a year before the American Declaration of Independence---it was, nevertheless, a product of the *collective genius of Europe*. The British, being the foremost representative of this new mode of production and in possession of a virtually unlimited domestic supply of its primary source of energy, namely, coal, *brought the industrial revolution to India.* And it was a two-way street, because a contributing factor to the rapid industrialization of Britain was undoubtedly the infusion of vast amounts of capital appropriated from India, coupled with the fact that India provided a huge market for Britain's industrial products.

There is ample evidence to support the view that the British did all in their power to impede the development of the new mode of production in India, preferring to preserve her as a source of raw materials, accessed and controlled through the large railway network, and as a market for goods manufactured in Britain. Indeed, to this end, the British often actively sought to destroy the many village-based medieval industries of India, namely, textiles, metal-working, glass, and paper, while simultaneously obstructing the introduction of new techniques. The inevitable consequence was to drive many people, who had formerly made their living from cottage industry, back to the land. India became progressively more ruralized. As Nehru notes in his book *The Discovery of India*:

> "In every progressive country there has been, during the past century, a shift of population from agriculture to industry, from village to town. In India this progress was reversed as a result of British policy. The figures are instructive and significant. In the middle of the nineteenth century, 55 percent of the population is said to have been dependent on agriculture, recently (prior to the second world war) this population was estimated to be 74 percent."

During the British period, India moved from being an assemblage of medieval states, some of them amongst the most advanced in the world, to becoming a united country that was amongst the most backward of modern nations. Meanwhile, many other countries not under the colonial yoke industrialized rapidly, most notably the United States. This industrialization was brought about in India only by the changing fortunes of the British during the First and Second World Wars. A whole generation of Britons, who might otherwise have sought their fortunes in India, perished instead on the battle-fields of Europe. The effective conduct of these wars, coupled with increased naval isolation of India from Britain, required that domestic production of basic items be undertaken in India itself and with substantial Indian labor. Only in this belated fashion did Britain contribute to the industrialization of India. And simultaneously Gandhi, armed with the *symbols* of medieval India, which he used so capably to capture the imagination of her down-trodden inhabitants, was able to capitalize on the weakened grip of the British and win India her freedom. Since then, freed from colonial restraints, India has made remarkable strides over the course of a half century in all areas of industrial production, and, in particular, in the information sciences and biotechnology.

In my opinion, the truly great contribution of the English to India was the infusion of a democratic spirit into her institutions. But here again I can only damn the colonialists with faint praise, because Britain did not give, in the true sense of that word, or even educate India into the ways of democracy. Only after the British departed in 1947 did India become a real democracy, under a newly-framed constitution and governmental structure patterned, in many respects, on the United States. Rather, Indian democracy was the outcome of a historical process that began in England, came to flower in the American colonies where it assumed a positively English character, and was later transmitted to the Indian colony during the period of British ascendancy, often against the will of the individual British rulers of the time. Indeed, I believe, but must hasten to add that it is a personal theory, that the American Revolution was an *English* revolution, a revolution nurtured by latent forces in England, but one that failed to take place in England itself. Support for such a view can be found, for example, in a February, 1987 article appearing in the *New York Review of Books* (italics mine), which states that

> "most historians now see the period between 1621 and 1720 as an epoch of continuous political turmoil, as England lurched unsteadily between tendencies towards royal absolutism on the French model and gentry-controlled anarchy of the Polish type, before settling down *to the eighteenth century* of aristocratic Whig control, of royal patronage and prerequisites, and *corruption and manipulation of a sharply reduced electorate,*"

and additional background and support for my argument can be found in *The Decline and Fall of the British Empire: 1781-1997*, a brilliant and monumental work by the University of Cambridge historian, Piers Brendon, which takes its cue from Gibbon's 18th Century masterpiece on the decline and fall of the Roman Empire. It is indeed fortunate that the American Revolution did occur in a distant virgin land, where it could flourish unimpeded by the forces of tradition and native culture, which inevitably return to suffocate change, as happened in France and later the Soviet Union. I also believe that the decline of England began with the American Revolution, much earlier than is usually assumed, and during a period when English power and invention were very much in evidence---recall that the industrial revolution began in England around 1775---because her spirit failed to keep pace with the political transformations taking place on the American and European continents. In effect, there were two Englands: on the one hand Imperial England, feudal in character, whose energies, thwarted on the American continent, were directed to India; and on the other, the England of a democratic spirit that gave birth to and indeed nourished the American Revolution.

It was the imperial face of Britain that Indians saw at home even as they found allies for the struggle for freedom in England itself. It is a phenomenon more easily understood when we observe the similar split personality in the United States of America, the leading superpower of today---democratic and restrained by her constitution at home, yet often dictatorial and supportive of some of the worst tyrannies abroad. Indeed, in many ways the United States has taken on the mantle of England, even to the extent of becoming the main shaping force of the English language. Viewed thus we are able to resolve many a political paradox. For example, victims of the death squads of South America that received the tacit support of governments propped up in the past by the United States, paradoxically came for safe haven to the United States itself. Under the protection of its constitution, they created an effective political platform for their cause, which helped to produce the much more democratic Latin America of today. This viewpoint helps us to understand also why Gandhi was so dear to the millworkers in Lancashire and to British intellectuals, both natural allies against the establishment, even as he was actively struggling to overthrow British rule in India. It serves to explain how Jomo Kenyatta, of whom we will have much more to relate in the next two chapters, was able to find a platform for initiating the fight for Kenyan independence in Britain itself in the nineteen-thirties. And it helps one understand the nature of the peculiar *love-hate* relationship that exists between the British and the Indian peoples. For even as we recognize the injustice of the British period, the history of India today is much interwoven with the remarkable people of the British Isles who ruled her for nigh on two centuries.

Throughout the long span of human history, there has been only a handful of what are known to anthropologists as *donor cultures*: Mesopotamia, ancient Greece, ancient India, China, England, and perhaps one or two others (arguably pre-Alexandrian Egypt, most certainly *not* ancient Rome). And, of these donor cultures, England's was one of the most remarkable. *To my mind, this is the true measure of England's greatness,* not the network of colonies that constituted the British Empire, on which it is said the sun never set. Admiration and love for English donor culture derives from a long list of contributions, some of which we have touched on in the foregoing discussion: England provided the lingua franca for the entire world; it was the birthplace of the industrial revolution; the root-stock or progenitor of the constitution of the United States and of modern democratic nations can be found in English parliamentary democracy; she gave us the foremost scientists (Newton, Darwin, ...), the greatest of dramatists and poets, great thinkers in other fields; England is home to two of the world's greatest universities; and so on. But, sadly, Britain chose then also to follow the path of ancient Rome, with all the attendant evils of empire, which has been a focus of discussion in this book.

It is a sad commentary on human nature that human beings everywhere, both rulers and ruled, will bow down ever more before the hate-engendering exercise of a greater power than they will before the love-inspiring achievements of a great culture.

Chapter 10

FIRST STEPS

The colony of Kenya, to which my parents returned after the Indian independence celebrations of 15 August 1947, remained firmly embedded within the British Empire. But, henceforth, newly-independent India would become a beacon of freedom for all the European colonies in Africa and Asia, and, in particular, a beacon for Goa, the small remaining Portuguese foothold on the Indian subcontinent, from which my grandfather had earlier emigrated, and which Portugal still adamantly refused to relinquish.

Three years earlier, following their wedding in Bombay in 1944, my parents had made their first home in Nairobi within a joint household on Forest Road where my father had lived, prior to marriage, with two of his siblings, his sister, Maisie, and his brother, Simon, an arrangement that they apparently found convenient to continue. For my mother, the transition from living safely within the bosom of her natal family to an entirely different environment on the other side of the Indian Ocean must have been a wrenching experience. Many years later, when she was nearing the end of her life, I asked her why she had chosen to make such a large adjustment to a new extended family and a strange new land

137

that required her, for example, to learn an entirely new lingua franca, Swahili, in order to communicate with the native people. My mother was not given to articulating her innermost feelings, although she felt them deeply, and she said very simply, "*I liked Mackie.*" So we must turn to another traveler, John Gunther, who in *Inside Africa* wrote extensively of his journey across the African continent during the early-1950s, in order to find words which might perhaps capture my mother's own first experience of her newly-adopted country just a few years earlier:

> "I suppose I liked Kenya better than any country we saw in Africa---politics aside. ...the magical combination of tropical climate and a piercing altitude, its exuberant frontier spirit, its extraordinarily dramatic beauty of landscape---above all the brilliantly blue, high, pellucid sky, with clouds pinned on it like clumps of chrysanthemum...... the country underneath, as we approached Nairobi [by air from the north], took on a peculiar intensity of colour, with sharp reds and spikes of savagely bright green. Even the trees glistened like bits of glass. There were green-tufted knobs and knolls, narrow twisting ravines, and steeply terraced farms. It was not surprising to learn later that the Kikuyu word for 'village' is 'ridge' because every community of round *bandas* (huts) is built sharply on its own prong of elevated land, and separated from its neighbours by rocky walls. The sun seemed to magnetize colours out of the raw earth; everything danced with an almost unnatural vibrancy. The impression was of a landscape in exaggerated form, like something looked at through a magnifying glass."

And what of the new extended family that my mother had joined after crossing the Indian Ocean? My paternal grandparents had died by that time and were buried in the cemetery at the foot of Forest Road, laid to rest under fine gravestones near that of a son, Gerald, whom they had lost at a young age. Thus my mother had exchanged her own parents, three sisters and a brother, whom we have met in a previous chapter, for her husband Mackie and his six siblings---my father's three sisters, Nathu, Maisie, and Clarice, and his three surviving brothers, Vincent, Eddie, and Simon--along with their spouses and their growing families of children. We will meet them all again in much more living color in *Up and About in Nairobi and Bombay*.

I was born in 1946, two years after my parents' marriage, while they were still resident in the shared house on Forest Road. A year after my birth, my parents travelled to India to attend the 1947 independence celebrations, of which we have already spoken, and upon their return to Kenya they too gained their independence by taking up residence in a little, rented house, also located on Forest Road and just half a mile down from the previous shared accommodation. This rental was owned by Aunty Nathu, my father's eldest sister, who resided in the house immediately adjacent within the same compound. Aunty Maisie and Uncle Simon also dispersed to separate households and the plot of land and the wood-and-iron house where they had lived together was sold. By coincidence, it was bought by the daughter of Dr. Rosendo Ribeiro---the pioneering figure whom we have met in a previous chapter---and her wealthy husband, and they promptly had the old wooden structure demolished and, in its place, erected an impressive, stone mansion.

My sister Jeanne was born in 1948 in the little rented house within Aunty Nathu's compound, and my brother Lionel followed two years later. With his birth in 1950, my parents' family was complete, and it was during the next decade, while we continued to reside on Forest Road in the little rented stone house under its maroon corrugated-iron roof, that my father's career in law and politics began to blossom and prosper. But before telling of his "golden decade" to come, let me give a brief portrait of the general context of our lives during that time.

Forest Road took its name from a narrow band of forest which receded as Nairobi progressively grew from a railway depot to the capital city of Kenya. One finds a vivid description of the state of this forested land and the local tribesmen during the early pioneering days, at the outset of the 20th century, in a little book written by L.S.B. (Louis) Leakey, the anthropologist who later was to attain considerable fame for his discoveries of prehistoric man in East Africa, and it is worth quoting verbatim from Leakey (1952) in our bibliography:

"By this time too there was only a narrow fringe of forest, varying from one to three miles wide, separating the open Athi plains, where the Masai pastoralists lived, from the Kikuyu agricultural lands that lay behind the fringe. [Recall the Masai and the Kikuyu were the two great and dominant tribes of Kenya.] Even the fringe itself---the forest belt---was already occupied and *owned* by Kikuyu families who had bought it from the Wanderobo [a primitive tribe of hunter-gathers whom we have also met in an earlier chapter]. This is shown not only by the evidence of the Kikuyu themselves, but also to the references to Kikuyu fortified villages, within the forest zone, by early travelers. The evidence is reinforced by the fact that the position of a big line of fortresses in what was then the forest fringe is known, and that where these fortified villages stood, huge middens of rubbish and broken potsherds of Kikuyu type can still be identified.

This forest fringe zone of Kikuyu land, with its fortresses, had a pivot point in the region of the Muthaiga suburb of Nairobi [this was, of course, the location of the notorious Muthiaga Club, which we have previously encountered---a curious coincidence!] and Ngara Road in Parklands, and ran from there along the high country bordering the plains towards the Ngong Hills [the residence of Karen Blixen] via the Langata Forest. On the other side it ran towards

Kiambu, Ruiru, and Thika. The object of the retention of this zone by the Kikuyu as forest was quite simple. The Masai on the plains were their traditional enemies and the zone with the fortified villages formed a kind of 'Maginot Line', which made raiding expeditions of the Masai much more difficult to accomplish successfully, and therefore enhanced the security of those living in the agricultural land behind the fringe."

Early European explorers of this agricultural region to the north of the forest describe it as *one vast garden* where the Kikuyu tribe, large in number, grew a wide array of crops---maize, sorgum, edible arum, bush peas, various beans, sweet potatoes, millet, bananas, and yams---and grazed their large flocks of goats and cattle, the monetary currency of pre-colonial times. But as Leakey later recounts:

"Most unfortunately for the Kikuyu and for the future relationship between the British and the Kikuyu, the position had materially changed by 1902 when the first alienation [European theft!] of the land for farming took place on a big scale. Four major disasters had ravaged the country in the interval; the great smallpox epidemic, the great rinderpest outbreak [a disease afflicting cattle], an intense drought with consequent famine and a devastating locust invasion. ……

As a direct consequence of these terrible events, the population was considerably reduced. No exact figures are available, for there was no census and estimates of death rate vary from 20 to 50 per cent. …… Land that had been under cultivation generally returned---as it does in Africa in a year or two---to bush, and by 1902 it could quite truthfully be said that it was being hardly used at all. …. This reduction of the population, however, did not in the least affect the *ownership* of the land."

Much of this recently-deserted land was allocated to European settler-farmers by the colonial Kenya government during the early decades of the twentieth century, thereby planting the seeds for the ensuing, decades-long conflict between the Kikuyu tribe and the white colonists.

By the time of my birth in 1946, the forest zone had dwindled to isolated tracts of woodland. The entire region, in particular the area to its south, which once was an unhealthy swamp through which ran the Nairobi River, had been transformed into an exceedingly pleasant colonial town. A complex mosaic of peoples now walked its bougainvillea-lined streets, separated in their daily lives by unseen walls defined by color, community, and religious faith. This was now a city of approximately 170,000 residents---15,000 white Europeans mostly of British origin, 45,000 brown Indians, and 110,000 black Africans, three-fourths being of the Kikuyu tribe---who occupied three parallel universes. Political power was essentially in the hands of the European settlers with nominal control from Britain. The Indians continued their centuries-old tradition of commerce. And the Africans provided the menial labor. Put another way:

Whites ran the show,
Browns minded the store, and
Blacks lived by the sweat of their brow!

In particular, in the residential districts that the surrounded the downtown area, most European and Indian households had one or more servants to do the household tasks: cooking, cleaning, and gardening. These areas were segregated by race, with Asians and Africans being barred from living in certain suburbs that were reserved for Europeans and also from the upscale European clubs and hotels. The Africans, mainly Kikuyu, had a particularly raw deal. The more fortunate were provided with rudimentary living quarters adjoining the homes that they served, but otherwise they found shelter in shanty towns on the outskirts of the city. In a book published in early 1954 by D.H. Rawcliffe, who had sought to open the eyes of the European settlers to the plight of the Africans and the roots of the Mau-Mau rebellion---we will have more to say on this soon---but instead found his book placed on the list of writings banned by the Kenya Government, one finds the following very illuminating paragraphs:

"The central reservoir of Kikuyu discontent has been the African slums of Nairobi---a natural consequence of the failure of the authorities to organize the social and economic development of the city along sound lines. As Mr. S.V. Cooke, the most liberal European member of the legislative council [this was governing body of Kenya popularly known as Legco to which may father was later elected] has said: "The existence of several shanty-towns within sight---and smell---of the town of Nairobi, is a devastating indictment of the Government and the municipality."

In their congested hovels Nairobi's African population live in abject conditions of squalor. Crime, disease, malnutrition and the insidious effects of widespread prostitution have reduced the people to a state of virtual amorality. ………

There could be no better breeding ground for crime and subversion than Nairobi's overcrowded hovels of 'bed-spaces'. In tumble-down shacks lit by oil-tins, in half-finished buildings, under parked lorries, the wretched Africans in the slums of Kenya's capital city had little to do except talk and argue over their grievances. To the Kikuyu living in their poverty-stricken shanty-towns, the relative wealth and luxury of the ruling white race, everywhere evident in the city's centre and suburbs, offered a fantastic contrast, evoking hopeless envy and sullen resentment all too easily exploited by political agitators."

In marked contrast to the local Africans, our family lived simply but comfortably in an Asian suburb of the town. Forest Road defined its northern boundary and ran roughly from west to east, its main segment, about a mile in length, stretching from the Church of St. Francis, past the nearby site of the shared household where my parents first lived, then a half-mile down past the rented house to which they had moved, past the cemetery where my grandparents lay buried, and then terminating in another Asian district called Pangani. At the church, the road branched off in four different directions. One went northwards towards Parklands and Muthaiga, leafy residential suburbs of large estates that were restricted to European ownership. A second branch went south towards the downtown area of Nairobi. And, in between, the other two branches defined boundaries of the church grounds. The northwest fork went uphill, out through the suburb called Westlands (this was the location of a mall where a disastrous terrorist attack by Somali Muslim extremists occurred many decades later), then followed a meandering, paved-over section of the old cart-road named for Sclater, which we've encountered in an earlier chapter, and eventually led out of town towards the Rift Valley and the White Highlands. The southwest fork at the church went up and then downhill, leading south to the Athi Plains and branching westward in the direction of the Ngong Hills to one of Nairobi's most outstanding features, the Nairobi National Park. Located barely a half-dozen miles from the town and criss-crossed by dirt roads, one could view dozens of species of free-roaming animals within the park from the safe confines of an automobile.

As for the downtown area of Nairobi, it lay well over a mile southwest of our home on Forest Road. Here were located the offices, shops, and hotels of the growing town, their low-lying buildings laid out on a grid-like pattern of broad, tree-lined streets. Two main avenues defined its "x" and "y" axes, so to speak. Government Road stretched from the railway station and across the downtown area, where it was lined with Asian-run shops, and it terminated at the Khoja mosque---the focal point of a prosperous, westernized Indian-Islamic sect headed by the Aga Khan---near the entrance to River Road, site of the first, burned-down Indian bazaar of a previous chapter. Many of the names of these shops belonged to Indian pioneers of the early days: Choitram and Sons, Alibhai Sharif, Kimji Bimji and Bros. (Nazareth Brothers could well have been one of them had my grandfather and granduncle not squandered their fortune.) A little way beyond the Khoja mosque was the site of the local institution of higher learning, the Royal Technical College at that time, later upgraded to university status. And next door to this college was the segregated Norfolk Hotel, which traced its history back to the pioneering days.

The other main axis of the town was Delamere Avenue, named for Lord Delamere, a British aristocrat and early pioneer of the colony, who had stood head and shoulders above all the other settlers of his breed. Its main section stretched from the western edge of the downtown area, which was defined by the Princess Elizabeth Highway, and terminated in a T-junction at Government Road. Delamere Avenue was actually three avenues, a main central road and narrower avenues on either side, separated from the main road by long, segmented islands, each several yards wide and planted with trees and tropical vegetation. Here was located the famous Stanley Hotel, named after the explorer whose notoriety was encountered in an earlier chapter. It was subsequently upgraded to the New Stanley, and like the Norfolk Hotel, it too was restricted to European-only patronage. No one would have expected then that, less than two decades after my birth in 1946, Kenya would become an independent nation, and that these two main avenues would be renamed for the first two African Presidents of Kenya---Delamere Avenue would become Jomo Kenyatta Avenue and, later, Government Road would be renamed Moi Avenue; and nobody would have guessed either that the

Norfolk and New Stanley Hotels would be desegregated and opened to all, or more accurately to the new ruling and moneyed class, because the Kenya then born anew has turned out to be not that different from the Kenya of old. To paraphrase the famous lines in a poem of William Butler Yeats: the beggar on horseback has become the beggar on foot, *but the lash goes on!*

In describing my family's living environment, we have encountered yet again the defining features of life in colonial Kenya---the extraordinary physical landscape, a highly unfair distribution of land based on race, and a color bar that resulted in the political and social life of Kenya being organized entirely along racial and communal lines. A chapter in my father's memoir, *Brown Man Black Country*, titled "A Glance at the Past" provides an excellent summary---one of the very best I've encountered---of these issues and the struggles in Kenya prior to his own involvement in politics, which began in 1944, the year of his marriage. By then he had paid off the huge monetary debt incurred for his legal education in England---the very last part was paid off with the dowry brought by my mother to the marriage---and my father was primed for the next phase of his life. In his memoir he describes his first, faltering steps into the political sphere as follows:

> "My entry into politics came about almost fortuitously. G.L. Vidyarthi, meeting me one day, asked me whether I was prepared to stand for election to the managing committee of the Nairobi Indian Association. Vidyarthi was a great supporter of Dr. De Sousa. He [Vidyarthi] was the nominal editor of the *Colonial Times*, the real editor and the writer of the editorials being generally believed to be Dr. De Sousa. In 1944 Dr. De Sousa was the President of the Nairobi Indian Association. When Vidyarthi asked me whether I was prepared to stand for election, I told him that I didn't think I stood any chance of being elected. I was quite unknown then. He replied:

"We'll get you elected." I agreed to stand. I doubt whether I had ever attended any political meeting before then.

So I attended what I believed was my first political meeting in Kenya. When my name was proposed very few hands were raised in support of this unknown Goan stranger. Whereupon Dr. De Sousa called out: "This is Mr. Nazareth, the well-known advocate," thus making it clear to his supporters who were present in force, that he wanted me elected. A forest of hands immediately shot up. I was elected. Such was my humble entry into politics."

My father was soon in the thick of Indian politics where he quickly learned that the central fissure within India itself, the tension between Hindus and Muslims, which would result a few years later in the partition of the subcontinent between an independent India and a newly-created Pakistan, was also a tectonic force within the Indian community in Kenya, one that was skillfully exploited by the British administration of the colony to keep the Indians divided. My father's election in 1944, soon after his entry into politics, to the Nairobi Commodity Distribution Board, a much coveted position at that time because of war shortages, was indeed to prevent an eligible but not well-liked or trusted Muslim, appropriately named Allah Ditta, from occupying it and, simultaneously, to avoid having to fill it with a Hindu. Being a Goan, my father was eminently qualified in this regard and was duly elected as the candidate that "split the difference."

The next two years were not a particularly active time for him within the political sphere, and it was only in September, 1946---as it so happens just a few months after my own birth---that he attended and participated for the very first time in a session of the East African Indian National Congress, the main political body of the Indian immigrants. To his surprise, he found himself catapulted into the position of honorary general secretary of the executive committee. This time, however, his unopposed election was "not on the stepping stone of differences between Hindus and Muslims," because several Muslims were elected to other positions. Rather it appears that the Indian community recognized his outstanding ability, most likely judged from his performance within the legal sphere, and considered him to be the most suitable man for the job. During his two-year tenure in that position, he recalls the three major issues facing the Indian community, namely, "Colonial No. 210 [a White Paper of the British Government] with its denial of equality of racial representation for the three main races [Europeans, Indians, and Africans], the demand for separate electorates by the Muslims, and the campaign by the Europeans to pass legislation to restrict or end Indian immigration." The situation was further complicated by the leaders of the Sikh community, who, encouraged by the Muslim separatists, also began to agitate for separate representation. The leaders of the Congress struggled manfully to keep Hindus and Muslims (and Sikhs) under the same political umbrella. At the next, biennial session of the Congress in August, 1948, my father's term as honorary general secretary came to an end, but he continued his meteoric advance by being elected, again without any significant opposition, to an office of vice-president, which he recalls had relatively little in the way of official duties. India and Pakistan had become independent nations a year earlier and the partition of the subcontinent was similarly reflected in Kenya by the Muslim leaders having left the Indian Congress to organize separately on their own. There were thus no Muslim aspirants for positions within the Congress and none was elected as an office bearer. My father was, in fact, the sole elected non-Hindu, but given his identification with the general body of the Indian community, which we have described in an earlier chapter, he had no feeling of being out of place. And so his rise concluded with his election to the Presidency of the Congress for its 20th session, which began with its next biennial congregation held in August, 1950 in the town of Eldoret, the heart of the so-called White Highlands. As my father describes it:

> "For the first time since its foundation in 1914, the congress was going to hold its session outside the major centers, Nairobi and Mombasa. In that sense, the session was historic. Naturally, there was tremendous excitement in the Indian community at Eldoret over this unique event in its history. Eldoret was then, one might say, the center where European race prejudice against Asians was at its worst. It was the center of the South African farmers, travelling in their ox-wagons from South Africa to settle in Kenya, who had ended their journey there and settled down to build farms in virgin territory."

He gave an impassioned Presidential Address at this Eldoret meeting of August 1950, which he began by quoting Nehru as follows:

> "Nowhere in the world can we accept a lower status for our people than the status of others. Nowhere will we approve of racialism or the suppression of one people or race by another. Indians abroad must remember that they have the honour of India in their keeping. That is a great privilege and a responsibility. Their honour involves fair and friendly dealings with the people of a country they go to. It involves also non-submission to wrong and injustice."

And, in a lengthy opening address, he continued in his own strongly-felt words:

> "Is it possible, or at any rate, is it easy, for the man discriminated against in his own country, in his home, to take pride in it? Can he say: 'I am a son of Kenya, and proud of it' and then with shame have to confess: 'But I cannot possess land in the Highlands. The Italians

and Germans who sought the destruction of my country may own land there, but I, who may be called upon to shed blood in its defence, may not?' Is he to say with pride: 'I come from that lovely land of Kenya, but in that homeland of mine, I may not enter European hotels solely because of the colour of my skin. Were I to attempt to enter one of these hotels on my own, I would be treated as an outcast, as one defiled. My birth or breeding, conduct or culture would be of no avail against the colour of the skin which God in his mercy has endowed me with and which He in his mercy has not placed in my hands the power to alter. The meanest European mechanic may enter, but I, be I a prince of rank and breeding, cannot?' And, so, if he declared his pride in his country, might he be led down a formidable and painful list. Is he to take pride in receiving three-fifths the European's pay for work equal to the European's? Or to rejoice that he is not allowed because of his colour or race to own or occupy land in certain parts of the town reserved to his fellow-subject with a lighter skin? It is not easy to be honestly proud of a second or third-rate citizenship. In an atmosphere charged with such deadly poison to the finer feelings, can the fine flower of loyalty or patriotism in all its luster bloom? Is he, who is forced to live in an atmosphere so oppressive, not driven to seek something, if he can find it, an ideal or maybe a country, more worthy of his love?

I speak of these things with feeling, for I was born in Nairobi and came back to it after my studies with the love of a young man. And since I came back, sixteen years have passed, while barred hotels and restricted areas, standing monuments of racial insult, and the many forms which the monster of race discrimination takes, have steadily drained the first flush of feeling out of me. I have taken this liberty of speaking of myself, for it is the epitome of many of you, born in this colony yet treated as strangers to it, almost as enemies, of whom this country should be home and has become almost a prison.

If only Europeans would take a little to heart the good old copybook maxim, 'Do as you would be done by' and put themselves in the place of the African and the Indian, they might realize the deep frustration and the seething discontent that is rife among the Africans and the Indians, the deeper and the stronger, the higher up in the scale they are, and they would then in large numbers, and not in ones and twos, come forward to labour and co-operate in a great joint undertaking, until the foul curse of racialism, which lies so heavily upon this continent, is lifted from our brows and this land has become a happy land for all, whose home it is to live for and to work for and, in this unquiet world, if need be when the time comes, to die for."

It was a fireworks display that gives some sense of my father's idealistic nature and it did not endear him to the European settlers, although it won the hearts of many Africans who heard it then or encountered its text later.

But this idealistic beginning came to nought during the two subsequent years when he worked strenuously on behalf of the Indian community, seeking to overcome the fracture between Muslims and non-Muslims and simultaneously to bring about constitutional reforms in the governance of the colony that would ensure a more equitable representation for both Indians and Africans. Despite vigorous protest from the mainstream of the Indian Congress, led by my father, the then-Governor of the colony, in co-operation with the Muslim leaders and, of course, the European settlers, pushed through the system of separate electorates based on religious affiliation, thereby widening the Hindu-Muslim rift and weakening the Indian community as a whole. New fractures then developed within the leadership of Congress itself in its efforts to address this changed political landscape, which are discussed in two lengthy chapters of my father's memoir, where he describes stormy meetings of the executive leadership. (During this period, he also organized one of the rare joint meetings held between the leadership of the Indian Congress and the Kenya African Union headed by Jomo Kenyatta, the future first president of an independent Kenya.) We will not go into any details here. Suffice it to say that my father's highly principled and yet pragmatic oppositional approach to the policies of the colonial government---a strategy of non-participation that he termed "blocking" the seats in the Kenya Legislative Council reserved for the Indian community, which was approved in a special session of the Kenya Indian Congress (KIC)---was itself thwarted by others within the KIC leadership who were willing to "cave-in," accept the partitioned electorate, and use it to their own advantage; and this capitulation, in turn, resulted in my father tending his resignation as President of the Kenya Indian Congress in April, 1952.

Being now out of political office and having control of his schedule as an independent barrister-at-law, my father took the opportunity to travel with the entire family to India on an extended visit, lasting from August, 1952, through December, 1952. While he was there he made one last-ditch effort on behalf of the Kenyan Indian community by securing a meeting with Prime Minister Nehru:

> "Nehru, when I met him in Delhi, was good enough to give me something like 40 minutes of his hard pressed time. He avoided all ostentation, going to the secretariat in a small car, a proceeding which in modern Africa would be absolutely infra dig, inconceivable to most even minor M.Ps [Members of Parliament].
>
> Nehru listened to me attentively, but very quietly, almost impassively, with scarcely any interruption. The subject to which I devoted most of my time was his practice of referring to Indians in Kenya as "guests." I tried to convey to Nehru that Indians living in Kenya fell into two classes: those who had made their homes in Kenya and

intended to remain there, and those who were birds of passage and who could rightly be referred to as "guests." I made it clear to him that he was doing Indians in Kenya a serious disservice lumping them all together and referring to them as guests.

From his silence or lack of any questioning or comment I came away from that interview feeling that I had been successful, and that he would desist from referring to us in Kenya as guests."

But perhaps Nehru's silence meant only that he felt Indians should identify completely with the African struggle for freedom and that those who did not should indeed be viewed as guests. Or perhaps he was simply aware that the Africans' struggle for freedom from British and white settler domination was entering an entirely new phase where the immigrant Indians would be forced to take sides, because in September, 1952, during the period when our entire family was away in India, the rebellion known as Mau Mau broke out into the open. In my father words, summarizing this event and the outcome of the first chapter of his political life, which had come to an end with his resignation from the Congress Presidency (italics mine):

"....on October 20, 1952, *Kenyatta* [of whom we will have much more to say in the next chapter] *was arrested and the country was plunged into the [Mau Mau] Emergency.* I remember I had met with Kenyatta about the time I decided to withdraw my name from the contest for the [next] Presidency [of the Kenya Indian Congress (KIC)]. He made no comment on my decision, but I thought I sensed a feeling of disappointment. *He might well have felt that under me the Congress would have given far more support and assistance to the African people in their day of tribulation* than under D.D. Puri [who followed my father into the office of President of the KIC]. By the time of the declaration of the Emergency, the Congress, the Indian elected members and the majority of the representatives of the Indian community had made themselves thoroughly ridiculous or despicable by unfailing or almost unfailing failure to adhere to any decision taken and by the fervent worship of many leaders of the seats in the Legislative council and the one seat in the executive council.

The history of the struggle of the Congress and of the majority of the representatives of the Indian community against religious separate electorates may be summarized in one sentence. *It was a story of discussions long prolonged, ending in resolutions bravely passed, followed by discussions long prolonged ending in stands cravenly abandoned,* "*much sound and fury signifying nothing.*"

The community had no inner strength capable of carrying out a strong or long struggle. Important leaders hungered too deeply for the fleshpots of Egypt. This story of consistent inconsistency ended fittingly with the reversal of the special session resolution on non-participation [as mentioned already, the thwarting of this resolution by others in the leadership had led to my father's resignation as President of the KIC].

It was conduct such as this by some prominent leaders that let down the Indian community miserably and brought the Congress into hatred, ridicule or contempt in the [eyes of the] African community. But the fault was not that of the Indian community. It was the fault of those who put themselves as its representatives."

Chapter 11

THE MAU MAU ERUPTION

In contrast to the weak and divided leadership of the Asian community, the white settlers of Kenya had strong, determined leaders who dominated the colonial government. Their racially-biased policies stifled all legitimate aspirations of the Kikuyu, the leading tribe of Kenya, and were directly responsible for the hidden build-up of pressure over the course of several decades, which was followed by a sudden eruption of violence in late-1952, akin to that of a volcano on the floor of the Great Rift Valley. The world came to know it by the dreaded name *Mau Mau*.

The roots of the tribe's deep discontent, as we have already seen, lay in their loss of land and the unraveling of a centuries-old, tribal way of life, which centered on webs of family ties and strong community obligations. Members of the tribe found themselves confined to a so-called Kikuyu Reserve, whose boundaries were drawn in a way that suited the needs of the government and the European settlers, and, outside this over-crowded area, they were reduced to the status of "serfs" on huge farms or ranches allocated to settlers in the White Highlands and on preserves set aside for forests. Otherwise, for lack of opportunity, they were forced to seek employment as servants in European and Asian households within the city of Nairobi, where they were provided with accommodation in tiny, servant-quarters attached to these (often palatial) homes or else they commuted to work from the abominable slums on the outskirts of the city. A few statistics concerning the economic and political landscape of Kenya in the early 1950s will highlight the inequities of the colonial system. They are taken from the commentaries of two distinguished and insightful observers who visited the colony during the Mau-Mau period.

The first of these observers, R.H. Rawcliffe, opens *The Struggle for Kenya* and sets the stage beautifully for his book as follows (italics mine):

> "About two-thirds of Kenya's 225,000 square miles are harsh and arid, the home of wandering bands of simple pastoral nomads as tough as the earth itself. The remaining third of the country is relatively fertile and contains about 90 per cent of the population of the colony. But even in this fertile area the land is of poor quality. In consequence the bulk of the population is concentrated within an area of some 52,000 square miles. Out of this about 35,000 square miles are reserved for the sole use of various African tribes. *In the midst of these tribes there lie 12,000 square miles of agricultural land which compose the 'white highlands'; in these no African [or Asian] may own land.*
>
> It is these 'white highlands' which have been a principal cause of the Mau Mau insurrection. The farms, plantations and ranches which constitute them are owned by some 3,000 Europeans, mostly British. All around them are the teeming populations of the African reserves where land-hunger is endemic.

The Europeans are not the only ones who have proprietary rights to huge areas of land. *The Masai, a nomadic, warlike tribe, about 55,000 strong, are in occupation of 15,000 square miles of poorly watered land over which they graze their innumerable cattle.* The Masai and the British have a great respect for each other, as is fitting for people of military renown who can keep the land they hold against all comers. [It is worth noting, however, that the Masai were moved by the government, not once but twice, in order to accommodate the settlers.]"

Rawcliffe continues:

"It has been recently estimated that there are about 5,300,000 Africans in Kenya. In addition to these there are over 120,000 Asians [Indians and Arabs] and about 40,000 Europeans. Of the African tribes the largest is the Kikuyu, which forms between a quarter and a fifth of the African population. It is this tribe which has brought forth the secret terrorist organization called Mau Mau and to which it has remained largely confined."

In other words, we have 12,000 square miles (of the best land) reserved for 40,000 Europeans of whom only 3000 were farmers and ranchers; 15,000 square miles (of poorly watered land) for 55,000 Masai; and *35,000 square miles available to 5,300,000 other Africans (including well over 1,000,000 Kikuyu for whom land ownership meant everything)*, and, dare we mention, 120,000 Asians.

The second observer, Fenner Brockway, was a socialist Member of the British Parliament, who visited Kenya in 1950 and again late in 1952. In his *African Journeys,* he provides the following bare statistics concerning the other face of the coinage of injustice, namely, the lack of political representation of the main racial groups (the terminology in this quotation is explained below):

"This is the present [in 1952] composition of the Legislative Council:

Race	Council of Ministers	Members	Population
Europeans	11	14	35,000
Asians	2	6	120,000
Africans	1	6	5,250,000
Arabs	-	2	20,000 "

The Legislative Council, or Legco as it was popularly called, was the governing body of Kenya and it was composed of "Members," some of whom were elected (within their respective racially-determined communities), whilst others were directly nominated by the Governor of Kenya Colony. (The latter was directly appointed by the British Crown, in effect, the Colonial Office in Britain, and considerable power was invested in his hands.) Likewise, some of the "Council of Ministers" were drawn from the ranks of the Members of Legco while others were nominated by the Governor, and the Executive (in effect, the Government) was composed of this Council of Ministers together with two additional Africans and one Arab. The complete domination of the Government by the very small population of Europeans is very evident from Brockway's foregoing tabulation.

We will not dwell here on other factors, for example, the inequities of pay scales and rates of taxation for the different races, in both government and private employment. But one cannot fail to mention, and it is impossible to overstate, the damage done to the African and immigrant Indian psyche by the *color bar*, the underlying rationale for the colonial system. We've spoken of it from the Indians' viewpoint in a previous chapter, via a quotation from my father's memoir, and Rawcliffe comments, equally eloquently, in his book's concluding chapter:

> "As long as the colour bar exists the problems of Kenya will remain intractable. No one who has discussed the subject with literate Africans can remain in the least doubt as to the truth of this simple fact. All reason and all argument are shattered against the mountain of resentment and frustration raised by colour prejudice. All the advantages and benefits of British government turn sour in the mouth of the African because of the *credo* of race superiority. The great underlying problem of Kenya is neither political, social nor economic; it is fundamentally psychological---a problem of attitudes, emotions and ideas which have no logical foundation.
>
> It is difficult for the European to comprehend the force of the resentment, amounting only too often to unreasoning hatred, aroused by the colour bar. One African put it to me this way: 'You Europeans can bring us every advantage that human beings have devised. You can be as kind to us as it is possible to be. You can come over here and develop our country, educate us, and provide money for our needs. But if while you are doing these things you consider you are too good for us, then we do not want anything from you; you can get out of Africa and stay out---and leave us to work out our own destiny.' "

These bare-bone facts alone serve to explain why Mau Mau was an inevitability. Indeed, the situation in Kenya in the early 1950s was in many ways reminiscent, indeed worse, than that in the U.S. American South during the same decade. And it is no accident that the sweeping away of the hated color-bar in the march up to Kenyan independence during the early 1960s coincided with the march for civil rights in the

United States, because such movements are often global in scope, although only recognized as such much later.

Who were the leading personalities behind the creation of the grossly inequitable economic, social, and political system in Kenya? If one were to single out two dominant and militant leaders of the Kenyan white-settler "tribe," as contrasted with patrician and scholarly notables in the Charles W. Hobleysian vein, for example, the renowned paleontologist Louis B. Leakey and the African specialist and author Elspeth Huxley, then surely the two names Hugh Cholmondeley, the Third Baron, who was known in Kenya as Lord Delamere, and Colonel Ewart Scott Grogan would come immediately to mind. Both were born within a few years of one another, Delamere in 1870 and Grogan four years later, and both came from privileged English backgrounds. Delamere was educated at Eton, an undistinguished scholar who inherited his title at age seventeen and then proceeded to roam the world. Grogan was a somewhat better student at Winchester, another well-known "public" school (private in the American sense). He went on to study law at Cambridge University, from which he was expelled---"sent-down" in the Cantabridgian vernacular---for tethering a goat within the rooms of his college tutor. (It would appear that the "sacrificial goat" was not restricted to the initiation rites of the Kikuyu tribe alone.) Their youthful imaginations no doubt fired by explorers like Speke and Burton, whom we have encountered in an early chapter, and, of course, by Cecil Rhodes, the white tribal Chief par excellence, both Lord Delamere and Ewart Scott Grogan undertook long treks across the African continent, each accompanied, one must not fail to note, by African scouts and porters to do the heavy lifting. (Much the same can be noted of the expeditions of Speke and Burton.) Delamere's adventurous spirit took him on shooting expeditions from the coast of Somalia and across northern Kenya into the region that later became known as the White Highlands, whilst Grogan's took him clear across the continent, from the Cape of Good

A PASSAGE TO KENYA

Hope, at Africa's southern tip, all the way up to Cairo. The Governor of Kenya at that time was eager to bring white immigrants of this calibre and pedigree to Kenya, and, as an inducement, Delamere was offered 100,000 acres of land in the northern highlands at a nominal rent and on a 99-year lease. Grogan obtained 64,000 acres of timber concessions along with part of Mombasa's deep water frontage on which he was able to later realize a huge profit. Enormously enriched in this manner, they both went on to become uncompromising, die-hard leaders of the white settler movement in Kenya, spearheading the policies that led eventually to the Mau Mau explosion of 1952.

The British are good at dressing up the ruthlessness of their colonial history, whilst pretending otherwise, and only recently has Great Britain as a whole begun to truly face up to its past. The first twenty years of the Protectorate, before Kenya became officially a colony around 1920, were the worst. We have seen Hobley's recounting of the subjugation of the African tribes in his memoir, and, in more recent writings, for example, the masterfully-written biography *Kenyatta* by Jeremy Murray-Brown, one finds the following (italics mine):

> "But the agricultural tribes were under increasing pressure from the settlers to provide labour. In 1908 confidential revelations over the conduct of government officers in recruiting labour for work on farms shocked the Colonial Office at a time when British opinion was critical of Belgian maladministration in the Congo [the very heart of darkness of the European colonies in Africa]. 'One might almost say', minuted one official in reading the report, 'that there is no atrocity in the Congo---except mutilation---which cannot be matched in our Protectorate'. By 1913 [the very year my father returned as a child to Goa] an official enquiry held in Nairobi into labour practices showed that settler attitudes towards Africans had not improved. To induce Africans to leave their own *shambas* [little agricultural plots in their

homelands] to work on European farms, *the majority of witnesses urged that compulsion of some sort should be employed---by increasing native taxation, or reducing native land areas, or simply thrashing those who refused to obey official requests for men.*

...... *Flogging, withheld pay, starvation, abandonment miles from food or shelter, disease, any one or all of these might be the lot of natives working for unscrupulous adventurers trying out the farming life.* One man supervised his workers from a chair, rifle in hand, which he fired at the feet of any one he thought was slacking.

There were, of course, many *good settlers* who were too busy on their farms to engage in the hot-house debates of Nairobi and who genuinely cared for their African labourers. But a single incident in the neighbourhood was enough to destroy a multitude of good deeds. One settler shoots a stock thief at dusk, another fixes himself up with native concubines, a third after a binge [of drinking] slaps an African bystander---and there's gossip in the markets, the old men shake their heads over their beer and the young men's anger rises. That was the atmosphere in which Kenyatta's generation of Africans grew up."

One of the less well-known facts about the pioneer era in Kenya was the disastrous impact of WWI (1914-18) on the African tribesmen. Here again we can quote from Murray-Brown, who describes this war as a watershed in Kenya's history, in particular, because WWI permitted the settlers, led by Ewart Grogan, to offer full-cooperation with the colonial administration in the conduct of the war in East Africa in return for being given a large say in domestic policy matters, in particular, over legislation involving land and native labor. He continues as follows in describing the aspect of the war that was in his view the most important, namely, its impact on the African (the statistics quoted below again speak for themselves; italics ours):

"The great need was for native porters. Warfare in the bush and jungles of East and Central Africa depended on long supply lines through appallingly difficult terrain. They could be maintained only by a constantly moving human chain. [One might note that the masters of the wheel did not have much use for it here.] Every territory throughout the continent was called on to provide men for this service.

Within a month of the start of hostilities, 5,000 men had been recruited. Depots were set up for the most populated tribes---at Kisumu for the Luo, Nairobi for the Kikuyu, and Mombasa for the Kamba and Swahili---and for the next four years an unending stream of men fed the troops at the front. Just how many Africans served as porters is impossible to say. *In some areas 75 per cent of the male population was taken off; in all, perhaps around 75,000 each from the Kikuyu and Nyanza provinces.*

The effect on African village life was devastating. Few ridges of Kikuyuland escaped the impact of recruitment into what were little more than slave gangs. Conditions in the camps and supply lines were appalling. The porters were badly fed, clothed and housed, and their ranks were decimated by the illnesses which overtook men [remember we are talking here about Africans not Europeans] unaccustomed to the tropical climate at low altitudes and unhygienic communal living. *The official death toll was put at 23,869. Reliable observers estimated twice as many.* To the number killed in action or from causes arising directly from the campaign must be added those who perished through diseases spread by the conditions of war. Among those the most devastating was the influenza epidemic of 1918-19 which swept through Kikuyuland and *accounted for 100,000 deaths among that tribe alone.*"

Following the war, Murray-Brown's aforementioned "good" settlers benefited greatly from the system put in place by the "bad" ones. Perhaps the *foremost spokesperson* to the outside world on behalf of the white settlers, good and bad, was Elspeth Huxley, whose parents brought her to Kenya in 1912 at the age of five (coinciding with Beryl Markham's arrival in Njoro and my father departure for India). The family settled as pioneer coffee farmers in Thika, near the headwaters of the Tana river, a few dozen miles northeast of Nairobi, in the direction of Mt. Kenya, and the first place to receive a branch railway from the city (in 1913). Elspeth Huxley, whose maiden name was "Grant" and who later married into the famous Huxley family in England, was a prolific author, writing altogether close to thirty books, but she is best known for *The Flame Trees of Thika* (subsequently made into a delightful TV series of the same name) and *The Mottled Lizard,* both based on evocative, albeit rose-coloured, memories of her childhood and teenage years in Kenya. They were published during the 1950s, long after Elspeth Grant-Huxley had left Kenya at the age of eighteen, in order to undertake her university education, first in England and later the United States. Thereafter, following marriage, Elspeth Huxley made her home in Great Britain, but she returned frequently to Africa. The aforementioned two books cemented her worldwide reputation as an author, but it is to her early writing that one must turn in order to obtain a better insight into her frame of mind, The most revealing of these is *Race and Politics in Kenya (1944),* based on a correspondence between her and (the Oxford Don and later Dame) Margery Perham, with an introduction by the liberal-minded Lord Lugard. The correspondence was initiated by Huxley on 10th March 1942, during the depths of WWII, and later published within the book's chapter "Invitation to Controversy":

> "When we met at the Colonial Conference you organized at Oxford last summer, you were kind enough to invite me to discuss with you, at some convenient time, the tangled problem of Kenya and its future. It looks now as if we shall never be able to meet for this purpose,

with so many war-time difficulties, transport and other things, in the way. I wonder if you would think it worthwhile to attempt some sort of a paper discussion? I suppose it would be a poor substitute for a proper face-to-face argument; on the other hand, one can often clarify one's ideas by setting them out on paper, so the time spent on the job mightn't be altogether wasted."

Margery Perham replied immediately on 15th March 1942 as follows:

"I am very glad you have written to me. There is no one with whom I would more gladly discuss the Kenya situation. Although I have met you only once, I have read all you have written---at least in your more serious hours!---with intense appreciation. Your *White Man's Country [: Lord Delamere and the Making of Kenya (1935)]*, apart from direct interest, is certainly the best apologia for white settlement that has been written, while *Red Strangers* [(1939); a novel imagining the life of generations of Kikuyu in the absence of European intrusion] is an astonishing exercise of sympathy and imagination on behalf of the Africans. I feel, therefore, that although you count yourself a Kenya settler, you will be able to put this controversial question into a wide perspective of our knowledge and experience. Having, as you say, been to Kenya to study its problems and having continued to read all I could of its records since my last visit, it will be a great stimulus to set my ideas beside your own and may help to clear my own mind."

And thus began a regular correspondence over the next year and a half, a full-throated confrontation between the "settler" and the "British liberal" viewpoints. The initial discussion addressed *past history, in particular, issues concerning land, labor, and taxation,* and Perham seemed to get the better of it. On 26th January 1943, Huxley, in a huff, proposed ending the correspondence on grounds that they were deadlocked in their review and interpretation of facts governing the past. But she quickly had a change of heart, writing again on 14th February to offer an olive branch and to propose a resumption of the correspondence even though, in sending the letter, "she was at risk of a snub." Two days later, Margery Perham replied magnanimously: "I am delighted that you have written to me again. I felt very unhappy about your breaking off relations, and I welcome the chance to go on groping with you through this tangled subject." They then continued over several more months, turning the discussion to the present and the future, and it is to their great credit that the entire correspondence was published in 1944 under joint authorship, with Lugard's introduction. It is impossible here to summarize this book, but no one who is interested in Kenyan history prior to WWII should fail to peruse their highly articulate correspondence in its entirety. (A notable omission, however, in this otherwise stellar material is the role of the Kenyan Indians, whose struggle against the European settlers and the colonial government was conducted in what could be termed a parallel universe.)

Lord Delamere died in 1931, three years before my own father's return to Kenya, and long before this settler-leader's life's work began to unravel following the Mau Mau rebellion and its aftermath. But Ewart Scott Grogan lived on in Kenya well into the Mau Mau era, although by then this larger-than-life individual, a "progressive settler" to some and an "appalling thug" to others, was a spent force. Fenner Brockway, the socialist M.P. mentioned above, who visited Kenya just before the outbreak of violence, recalls their first meeting in Kenya, near the end of Grogan's life. The aged Colonel apparently reveled in telling Brockway how he was offered "grilled baby by a cannibal tribe" on his epic trek across the African continent, but seemed to have little to say about the politics of the time. However, he left a memoir (with Arthur H. Sharp) penned much earlier, *From the Cape to Cairo (1900)*, in which he describes his adventurous exploits. Two quotes from the book's introduction and its closing chapter, respectively, will provide a clear window into Grogan's distorted thinking (italics mine):

> "To the probable objection that I have devoted too much attention to the sporting side of our trip, I would answer that *were it not for the big-game shooting, for no earthly consideration would I put my foot one mile south of the pyramids.*"

Indeed Grogan's memoir devotes an inordinate number of pages to the senseless slaughter of wild animals, purely for "sport" in the vein of Samuel Baker and John Speke, the 19th century explorers of whom we have spoken earlier (see Chapter 2). The second quote is from Grogan's concluding chapter titled "Native Questions":

> "The enormous extent of Africa and the consequent infinity of tribes widely divergent in origin, character, and habits, makes it almost impossible to generalize on this most abstruse subject. Still some principles may be laid down for the great negroid population of Africa which, as far as my experience goes, apply in most instances. I will ignore Biblical platitudes as to the equality of men irrespective of colour and progress, and take as a hypothesis what is patent to all who have observed the African native, that he is fundamentally inferior in mental development and ethical possibilities (call it soul if you will) to the white man.
>
> He approaches everything from an entirely different standpoint to what we do. What that standpoint is, what his point of view is, by what mental refraction things are distorted to his receptive faculty, I cannot pretend to explain. I have failed to find any one who could. But the fact remains that if a native is told to do anything, and it is within the bounds of diabolical ingenuity to do it wrong, he will do it wrong, and if he cannot do it wrong, he will not do it right. I can but

suggest as an explanation that he is left-minded as he is generally left-handed. The following anecdotes will illustrate my meaning. They all come under my personal observation, and tend to show the impossibility of following a native's reasoning, if he does reason."

The remainder of the chapter must be read in its entirety by anyone interested in a written record of the unshakeable, indeed irrational prejudice of men such as Grogan, who often held sway over the unfortunate masses in Great Britain's former colonies across the globe. One of his primary objectives was to scout a possible route for the Cairo to Cape railroad across the continent envisioned by Cecil Rhodes. His journey thus took him through the western arc of the Rift Valley (described in Chapter 2) and, often by boat, across its series of lakes, down the passage of the Nile River through the morass of the Sud (also described earlier), and eventually into more well-travelled regions of the Sudan and upper Egypt, a relatively small topographical sample of the vast African continent. And this small sample was matched by the *minuteness* of the sample of individuals upon which Grogan based his all-to-sweeping generalization---primarily the motley collection of porters who, presumably for want of other ways to make a living, were enlisted to carry his heavy baggage of guns and supplies and, when it was disease afflicted, even his physical body, and who thus may not have been inclined towards full cooperation.

In response to these two dominant leaders of the white settlers, the Kikuyu tribe threw up two formidable leaders of their own: Harry Thuku and Jomo Kenyatta. They were roughly the same age---Thuku was born in 1895 and Kenyatta's birth date is unknown and placed sometime between 1890 and 1897 by his biographer, Murray-Brown---and initially their lives followed parallel courses. Both encountered their first white man in the early 1900s, they both had the wherewithal to seek as much elementary education, namely, basic reading and writing, as was available to them within the religious missions, and both elected to be baptized into the Christian faith, while simultaneously taking care to undergo initiation into full stature within the Kikuyu tribe through its circumcision ceremony. Afterwards, in early adulthood, they both were able to secure what might be considered "plum" jobs---relative, of course, to what was available to the majority of their tribe and humble in every other way. However, unlike Delamere and Grogan, their two white-settler counterparts, these two African leaders of the future possessed very different temperaments from each other, and eventually their life-paths diverged greatly.

Harry Thuku began adult life by "sweeping and dusting tables, and carrying out messages" for a bank. Later, at the onset of WWI, he landed a "plum" job as a compositor of type and a machine operator at a newspaper, the *Leader of British East Africa*, where he made himself invaluable by learning how to print maps and sketches of war positions, thereby avoiding forcible recruitment to fight the Germans in East Africa. War nevertheless brought out Thuku's fighting spirit as he became increasingly aware of the treatment and plight of his fellow Africans. Many years later, over a three-week period with twelve whole-day sessions undertaken shortly before his death, Harry Thuku orally communicated his autobiography to the historian Kenneth King, who then transcribed, edited, and published it posthumously in Thuku's name. The deep grievances of the African are communicated here in a milder way than one might perhaps expect, and the chapter titled simply "Nairobi," from which they are now quoted, should be read in its entirety in order to sense the spirit of the man (italics mine):

> "It was at the *Leader* [a newspaper that served the interests of the white settlers], from about 1915 [just two years after Elspeth Grant-Huxley's parents had arrived as settlers in Kenya], that I began to think seriously about some of our troubles as Africans---*especially this*

question of forced labour. Before then [the onset of WWI] only men had been made to work, but about that time women and girls too were compelled to go out to work. This was what happened: a settler who wanted labour for his farm would write to the D.C. [the white District Commissioner] saying he required thirty young men, women or girls for work on his farm. The D.C. sent a letter to a chief or headman [African tribesmen put in place by the government---perhaps this very D.C.---and subject to its will, serving to enforce a system set up to hold the natives in check] to supply such and such a number, and the chief in turn had his tribal retainers to carry out this business. They would simply go to people's houses---very often where there were beautiful women and daughters---and point out which were to come to work. Sometimes they had to work a distance from home, and the number of girls who got pregnant in this way was very great. But I shall say later what I tried to do about this."

Forced labor ended around 1921 in the aftermath of WWI, but was replaced by the hated "*kipande*" system that was in effect throughout the colonial period. Thuku describes this in detail and its consequences for the African, picking up a theme already sounded above (italics again mine):

"First there were many thousands of porters who came back from very difficult conditions in the East Africa Campaign [as we have discussed above], and found that they would not get any gratuity. Instead the government under General Northley decided that the white soldiers, especially the officers, should be rewarded. So they alienated many thousands of acres in the area around Kericho [roughly three-fourths of the distance, as the crow flies, between Nairobi and Kisumu (on Lake Victoria)] for a Soldier Settlement Scheme. Also in my own Kaimbu area [in the heartland of the Kikuyu homeland] more land was taken at this time and given to white settlers. However, I want to make one thing clear about this land business; ... what we objected to was that the Europeans did not treat us as we had treated the Dorobos [Wanderobo tribe]. I mean, we bought the land from the Dorobo according to agreed prices ...we did not simply claim the land without the Dorobo knowing anything about it ...

The second thing that was making Africans angrier after the War [WWI] was this thing called *kipande*. This was Swahili for a container in which a registration paper was carried. Now General Northley, Kenya's Governor after the War, decided in 1919 to implement the recommendations of an earlier committee which had suggested that Africans be registered. The ordinary people did not understand what this registration was, but even more educated ones like me did not oppose it to begin with, for we knew that many countries asked their citizens to register. So we did not object until we found out that it was a very different business in Kenya. First of all you had to wear this quite heavy metal box round your neck on a string all the time [photographs of a kipande and its contents can be found in Thuku's autobiography]; then in the columns inside there were many things that were against Africans. There was one space that the employer had to sign when he engaged you and also when you left. You could not leave employment without permission and if you did, you could be taken to the D.C.'s court [District Commissioner, one of the enforcers of the colonial system]. Also, no other employer would take you if the space of discharge was not filled up. Another thing in the early kind of *kipande* was a space for remarks; and here, if the employer did not like you, he could spoil your name completely by putting 'lazy', 'disobedient', or 'cheeky'. That column made me very angry. *Kipande* was only for Africans; and in 1919, at that old building still standing opposite Nairobi General Post office, I collected my one.

There was also the question of rising tax for Africans. It kept on going up even though we did not see anything like schools or clinics which we get nowadays for our high taxes. The reason for it was to pull African workers out of their houses to work for the European settlers; you see, they could not get the money to pay their tax unless they left their homes and worked for some months. Then also there was the confusion when the currency changed from India rupees to shillings. *Colonel Grogan, Lord Delamere* and Mr. Archer, the settler leaders, brought this change because they thought the Indians were secretly exporting rupees to India---hidden in large tins of ghee! [all the better to grease palms as well]. The new rate was one old rupee equals two shillings, but many people tried to give Africans one shilling for one rupee. I was all right, for in my government job, I had got 70 rupees, and this now gave me Sh. 140/-.

The final thing was when we heard that the settlers were going to reduce *African wages* by one third. Many of us got very angry, and we called a meeting in Pangani on 7 June 1921 to see if we could form a Young Kikuyu Association [(YKA)]. ......"

Thus began a period of peaceful organizing and petitioning of the Colonial Office. Thuku proceeded over the heads of the "loyalist" chiefs of the tribe, who were seen as stooges of the local government, and he thereby rapidly attained a leadership position among the Kikuyu. He had many friends, even mentors, among the Indian immigrants in Kenya, and he viewed Indians and Africans as being on the same side in the struggle for political and economic rights. Unlike Kenyatta, he was not "Kikuyu to the core," and, in order to broaden the movement's appeal to other tribes as well as to the Indian immigrants, he even changed the name of his organization from the aforementioned Young Kikuyu Association (YKA) to the East African Association (EAA). For his political efforts, Thuku soon earned the enmity of both the loyalist African tribal chiefs and the local white settlers, and, on March 14, 1922, he was arrested and held in a police station in Nairobi. A demonstration by his supporters outside numbered in the thousands and, after it turned disorderly, the demonstrators were fired on by the police, resulting in many deaths. The EAA was promptly proscribed as a political organization and Thuku was deported to a distant outpost, and thereafter he was held in detention *without trial* for a full eight years. Although not mistreated, this long period of detention served to dampen his youthful political fervor—it was during this time that he found his true calling as a "gentleman farmer"---and also to sideline his leadership role within the Kikuyu tribe. Its allegiance began to shift to Jomo Kenyatta, the central, transformative figure of Kenyan politics, whose life-trajectory spanned the entire six and a half decades of colonial rule, and whose political destiny was deeply intertwined with that of his Kikuyu tribe.

At the time of Harry Thuku's removal from the political sphere in 1922, Kenyatta was himself in possession of a "plum" job available to Africans. As described by his biographer Murray-Brown, he was employed as an assistant to the water superintendent in the Public Works Department, with official duties as a "stores clerk and meter reader," and at an unusually high salary (again for an African). He proceeded to build a house for himself and the wife whom he had earlier married and who had borne him a son, he invested in a bicycle, bought better clothes, and "in this obscure corner of the British Empire … enjoyed the jazz age of the twenties." Well aware of Thuku's fate, he was careful to maintain a low political profile, and only gradually did he become active within the Kikuyu Central Association (KCA), the organization newly created to fill the vacuum left by the banning of Thuku's EAA. The Kikuyu soon recognized Kenyatta's ability and qualities of leadership and, in 1929, the KCA selected him as its chosen representative to air its grievances before the Colonial Office in London, in particular, to present to the Secretary of State a petition on native land rights, the release of Harry Thuku from detention, and other matters. Kenyatta leapt at this opportunity to further his education and explore much wider horizons and he quickly booked passage to England, even though an interview with the authorities in London was by no means guaranteed. He then managed to remain abroad for the next eighteen months, a time of enormous personal growth for him, during which he made key contacts with liberals within the Labor Party, undertook a side-trip to Moscow, wrote pamphlets, and published letters in newspapers. Perhaps most significantly, he found a mentor in W. McGregor Ross, becoming almost a member of his family. Ross was a prominent member of the Labor Party and earlier had spent two decades in Kenya. In his capacity as Director of Public Works, the very department where Kenyatta had once found employment as a water meter reader, Ross had helped to oversee Nairobi's growth from a railway depot to a colonial capital. In particular, he had laid out a broad avenue that ran the length of the town, initially called simply 5th Avenue, later renamed for Lord Delamere, and, in an ironic twist of fate, eventually renamed for the first president of an independent Kenya, Jomo Kenyatta. But all that lay far in the future.

One of Kenyatta's letters, which was published in the *Manchester Guardian* of March 18, 1930, shows clear evidence of tutelage by Ross. It is remarkably prescient of the Mau Mau explosion that was to come two decades later and is best quoted in its entirety (italics mine):

"Sir: May I be permitted to throw some light on the so-called "unrest among the Kenya natives:"

I should mention in passing that I am a Kikuyu, and, with all public-spirited men of my tribe, regard with considerable uneasiness the policy that is being advocated by certain influential people, both in Kenya and in this country, of further alienating our land from us, for the use of non-natives, in conjunction with attempts to abolish wholesale our tribal customs. General Smuts has recently condemned most wholeheartedly a similar policy which is being carried out in South Africa.

The Kikuyu Central Association, of which I am the general secretary, is not a subversive organization. Its object is to help the Kikuyu to improve himself as a better Mu-Kikuyu, not to "ape" the foreigner. Our aims and object may be summarized briefly under the following five headings:

1. LAND. – To obtain a legal right, recognized by the local government, to the tenure of lands held by our tribe before the advent of the foreigner, to prevent further encroachment by the non-natives on the native reserves.
2. EDUCATION. – To obtain educational facilities of a practical nature to be financed from a portion of the taxes paid by us to the government.
3. WOMEN'S HUT TAX. – To obtain the abolition of the 'hut tax' on women, which leads to their being forced into work outside the native reserves or into prostitution for the purpose of obtaining money to pay the tax.
4. REPRESENTATION IN THE LEGISLATURE. – To obtain the representation of native interest in the Legislative Council by native representatives elected by the natives themselves.
5. TRIBAL CUSTOMS. – To be permitted to retain our many good tribal customs, and by means of education to elevate the minds of our people to the willing rejection of the bad customs.

Evolving from these five points we hope to remove all lack of understanding between the various people who form the population of

East Africa, so that we may all march together as loyal subjects of his Britannic Majesty along the road of Empire prosperity. I would like to ask if any fair minded Briton considers the policy of the Kikuyu Central Association outlined above to savour in any way of sedition? The repression of native views, on subjects of such vital interest to my people, by means of legislative measures, can only be described as a short-sighted tightening up of the safety valve of free expression, *which must inevitably result in a dangerous explosion – the one thing all sane men wish to avoid.*"

What more reasonable set of demands could there be? There is no mention of independence, not even the hated "kipande." But Kenyatta's tone was more strident in letters that he sent to *The Daily Worker*, a socialist newspaper, reflecting his short sojourn in Moscow and perhaps his deeper feelings. He was ever a man to hold his cards closely to his vest, ever the master of ambiguity, often willing to alienate his mentors, not averse to biting the hand that fed him. Perhaps he was already well aware that the "liberal" perspective of the above-quoted letter, akin in spirit to that of Margery Perham and an expression of Great Britain's democratic face when turned towards the homeland, was incompatible with her colonial policy abroad, the authoritarian face of Great Britain that we have considered in some detail in Chapter 10. Perhaps he knew already that the "dangerous explosion" of the letter's conclusion was inevitable.

In September, 1930, Kenyatta returned to Kenya. But, shortly thereafter, he was selected for a second KCA representation to London and, ever mindful of the risk of being detained without trial by the colonial administration, he leapt at the opportunity to once again go abroad. By that time, Harry Thuku, the still widely-acknowledged leader of the Kikuyu tribe, had been released from detention, but his movements continued to be restricted by the authorities and he was not permitted to travel to London to represent the KCA. Sadly, Harry Thuku's sun was already beginning to set.

In May, 1931, the year of Delamere's death, Kenyatta booked passage on an Italian liner in Mombasa and set sail again for Europe, marking the beginning of a peripatetic, self-imposed "exile" that lasted this time for a decade and a half. In England he lived by his wits and by the sheer force of his personality, perpetually short of funds, often dependent on the largesse of others. Again he made new contacts, in particular, with other young African and African-American activists. He somehow found means for travel in Europe, returned to Moscow for an extended visit, made a little money on the side as an extra in a movie starring Paul Robeson with whom he struck up a friendship; and, in full accord with his Kikuyu heritage, he later took a second wife, an Englishwoman, who also bore him a son. But during this extended absence from Kenya, by far the most important relationship that he developed was with the world-famous anthropologist, Professor Bronislaw Malinowski, on which his biographer, Murray-Brown, insightfully comments as follows:

> "Kenyatta attended Malinowski's classes for something like two years. The two men apparently became close friends. They shared certain prejudices, among them a dislike of Indians [in marked contrast to Harry Thuku]. 'My lectures are not for Indians' Malinowski was known to open a session, and Kenyatta would follow up by describing how Indians exploited Africans in Kenya [according to Prince Peter of Greece who also attended Malinowski's classes and with whom Kenyatta also struck up a friendship that introduced him to an aristocratic, cosmopolitan world in London and Paris]. Malinowski's classes included names subsequently famous in the field of anthropology ….. as well as African specialists like Elspeth Huxley who later wrote [in an article published around the time of Kenya's independence] that

Kenyatta was 'one of Dr. Malinowski's brightest pupils....A showman to his fingertips; jovial, a good companion, shrewd, fluent, quick, devious, subtle, flesh-pot loving.....'"

It was during this time that Kenyatta gathered together the material for his extraordinary book, *Facing Mount Kenya,* which was published in 1938. It was both a well-constructed anthropological work on the Kikuyu tribe, and, more importantly, a masterful political manifesto that sought to contrast a mythical, golden-age of the Kikuyu, before the arrival of the white man, and the tribe's degraded condition under colonial rule. In assembling the book from his written and oral presentations in Malinowski's classes, Kenyatta apparently had the assistance of a gifted, Oxford-educated English activist, Dinah Stock, who helped with the ordering of his seminar essays, correcting their English and spelling. But her editorial contribution and Malinowski's mentoring in no way detract from the book being, in its essence, entirely Kenyatta's; just as Beryl Markam's memoir, *West with the Night,* is truly her own, the rumored assistance of her husband notwithstanding (as we have discussed in Chapter 8); just as the poems of T.S. Eliot's belong entirely to him, despite the well-known editorial hand of Ezra Pound. Jomo Kenyatta's book served to solidify his identity and simultaneously to fulfill a political objective, and a more recent analogue can be found, perhaps, in Barack Obama's *Dreams from My Father.* He had created his "burning spear"---a designated English translation of "Jomo", a name that was itself invented—and now he awaited his moment for its thrust forward, into the body politic, in the fight to free his people.

Men of destiny like Kenyatta know instinctively when the moment is ripe. After the end of WWII (1939-45), he must have sensed that Great Britain was a spent force. A generation of Britons who might otherwise have sought their fortunes in the Empire had instead perished on the battlefields of Europe. Indian independence was just a year away. In September, 1946, coincidentally the year of my birth, he chose to return to Kenya, where his name was already legend among the Kikuyu and where he received a hero's welcome. Soon he was leading the Independent Teachers' Training College (part of the mission-independent schools' movement) and enjoying a comfortable life in the Kikuyu heartland. In mid-1947, he was elected President of the Kenya African Union (KAU), a reincarnation of the KCA which the government had banned as a subversive organization at the start of WWII. One can get a good sense of this pre-Mau Mau period in Kenyatta's life from Fenner Brockway's aforementioned *African Journeys* (its author was another one of Kenyatta's left-leaning contacts in England), which was based on visits to Kenya in 1950 and 1952. The chapters on Kenya are a quick and easy read and well worth perusing. One paragraph describing Brockway's visit to the Teachers' College is particularly striking (italics mine):

> "In a distant corner [of the "college campus"] were Kenyatta's headquarters, the most elaborate thatched hutment I had seen in Africa, the thatch and walls flawless, large rooms, library, bedroom, kitchen, furnished tastefully and comfortably. There were shelves crowded with books, anthropological, historical, social, political, with a strong bias towards Marxist works. On the walls were photographs of Lenin, Paul Robeson, and Nehru. Jomo was proud of his library, and as he took one after another from the shelves and pressed them back he spoke with a genuine love of his books. *I liked him more at this moment than I had ever done.*"

The journalist and world-traveller Negley Farson, of whom we have also spoken in a previous chapter, had likewise met Jomo Kenyatta not long before (at the end of 1947) and he records the following impression of an inscrutable man who was, at that time, already in his mid-fifties:

"A big, paunchy man, bearded, with slightly bloodshot eyes, a theatrically monstrous ebony elephant-headed walking stick, a gold-rimmed carnelian signet ring about the size of a napkin-ring, an outsize gold wrist-watch fastened to his hefty arm by a gold strap, dressed in European tweed jacket and flannel slacks---with as pleasant, ingratiating and wary a manner as you have ever met. He has a series of grunts – "UNH-HUNH!" – whose rapidly switching inflections might mean anything. He struck me as being a born actor, an evident leader, and, perhaps just because of this, a man born for trouble."

During the post-WWII period, the Mau Mau movement had been building pressure, slowly and secretly, like magma within a volcano, whilst outwardly, on the earth's outer crust so to speak, the KAU was officially pursuing constitutional methods. However, it was riven by differences between the moderates and the "young Turks." Many among the latter had been recruits and had fought on the side of the Allies during WWII, and in particular had experience of guerilla tactics in South-East Asia, and they now became the driving force behind the building Mau Mau movement.

The origin of the word Mau Mau itself is unclear and perhaps the most plausible explanation is given by J.M. Kariuki, a young Kikuyu activist, in his book *'Mau Mau' Detainee:*

"Few people seem to know the origin of the name 'Mau Mau'. Kenyatta said time and time again that he did not know these words nor did his people. ....

This is the real origin of the name 'Mau Mau'. Kikuyu children when playing and talking together often make puns and anagrams with common words. When I was a child I would say to other children 'Ithi, Ithi', instead of 'Thii, Thii' (meaning 'Go, Go') and 'Mau, Mau' instead of 'Uma, Uma'.

One evening when an oathing ceremony was being held, the guard who kept watch outside was told to utter this meaningless anagram as a warning to escape in case the police or some other enemy approached. That night the police did visit the house, heard the warning being shouted, found the house empty and reported back that they had heard the words "Mau Mau" which thereafter became attached to the oath of unity although not the movement itself. But he then continues (italics mine):

> "I [Kariuki] have been told that the name 'Mau Mau' was used soon after by a Rift Valley Kikuyu called Parmenas [Parmenas Kiritu was a Protestant Christian leader of a group of 'loyalist' Africans]........ When Parmenas began to hear about the new movement and the oath which was used, he considered that it was anti-Christian. He therefore began to speak out against it in his sermons. Parmenas knew how Kikuyu children sometimes shouted the anagram 'Mau Mau'. He made use of this traditional habit to pour scorn on the movement as a childish thing. Then many people who did not know about the Society started to use these words which spread over the country.
>
> I must make it clear that it [this new Kikuyu movement] did *not have any special name;* the world knows it by a title of abuse and ridicule with which it was described by its bitterest opponents. [Nowadays, it is common practice to use the name Land Freedom Army (LFA) and describe its members as 'freedom fighters.']"

And thus, much like the invented name "Jomo," as already mentioned above, the name "Mau Mau" too was a Kikuyu-word construct.

It is difficult to assess precisely how much Kenyatta himself knew of these growing, subterranean developments, how much he looked the other way, how much of their activities he actually condoned, where he stood on the line between "moderate" and "extremist." His dilemma and the growing intertribal conflict came to a head in 1952, a pivotal year in Kenya's history, and is described by Murray-Brown as follows (italics mine):

> "The pressures on Kenyatta [as President of the KAU] mounted. KAU was now virtually in the hands of the younger men in Nairobi. In January 1952 they formed their own secret Central Committee and began building up a network of subordinate secret cells throughout Kikuyuland. They used Kenyatta's name freely in their propaganda, which included a stepped-up program of oathing. They made secret plans for armed rebellion. A tariff was placed on any arms and ammunition collected. *Some Indians [most notably a Goan named Pio Pinto] played important roles as suppliers.* ...
>
> Anyone suspected of betraying information to the administration was murdered. ... African police disappeared, sometimes without trace, sometimes with a limb inadvertently left behind after dismembering. Bodies turned up in rivers, some tied with wire. Women were stripped and beaten if they did not co-operate by taking the oath or otherwise helping the movement. The atmosphere grew heavy with fear, suspicion, and hatred. Despite Kenyatta's attempt to make KAU inter-tribal, the Kikuyu were cutting themselves off from the rest of the Africans in Kenya, and the moderates among them were isolated. Tribal morale was disintegrating."

Shortly after Mau Mau broke out into the open in the second half of 1952, a state of emergency was declared by the colonial government, and Jomo Kenyatta, along with several other KAU leaders, were arrested. Unlike Harry Thuku, Kenyatta was put on trial at the end of that year and, although ably defended by lawyers brought from England and India, his conviction was a foregone conclusion. He was thereafter placed in *the preserving formaldehyde of detention* for a period that extended into the next decade, and once again he was to patiently await the call of destiny. Others leaders of the KCA being similarly convicted, any moderating force over the Mau Mau movement was removed. Earlier, the colonial authorities *begat* Jomo Kenyatta by detaining Harry Thuku. Now, by detaining Jomo Kenyatta and other moderates, they begat much more extreme Kikuyu leaders, who were waiting in the wings to take their place, and Mau Mau continued on its deadly course over the next two years (1953-1955).

The book *Mau Mau and the Kikuyu* by the distinguished paleontologist L.S.B. Leakey was published in 1952, soon after the emergency was declared. Leakey had been working on a definitive, multi-volume anthropological work on the Kikuyu tribe, and, when Mau Mau broke out, he appears to have rushed into print this little book that was every bit an effort at myth-building, a marshalling of facts and arguments to support a political objective, as was Kenyatta's *Facing Mount Kenya*. It would not be unfair to describe Leakey as a reincarnation of John Boyes, albeit a much more benign, literate, and accomplished version of that rapscallion. Leakey had grown up in Kikuyuland, the son of Christian missionaries, and he was fluent in the difficult Kikuyu language. In fact, he had been made a member of his Kikuyu age-group and later a tribal elder, a rare tribute given to only a few. It is said that Leakey had once attended a presentation by Kenyatta at one of Malinowski's classes in London and that afterwards the two got into a shouting match *in the Kikuyu language*. Like Elspeth Huxley, who also grew up with Kikuyu playmates, Leakey had a very large blind spot: his diagnosis ignores, in the main, the economic and political roots of Mau Mau, and, true to his own missionary heritage, he chooses to focus instead on demographic, social, spiritual, and even linguistic causes as typified by the following (italics mine):

"In the days before the British came to Kenya, the rate of population increase was kept at a low level because, in addition to periodic epidemics such as smallpox, there were two other limiting factors operating. One of these was the very high infant mortality rate and the other the Kikuyu rule which forbade a woman to start a new child until the one she was suckling was weaned [so that the spacing of infants was roughly three years]. .... Had these two factors affecting the increase in population continued in operation after the inhabitants of the Kiambu part of Kikuyu country had been so drastically reduced by famine and smallpox at the end of the last [19th] century, the population would still be small today and most of the land problems and land hunger which are causing so much concern now would not exist."

:

"Not being very mature in political matters, the leaders of the K.C.A. in 1922, and during the next few years, did not realize that their best chance to achieve some redress would be to make a *well-argued* case and present it to Government through constitutional channels. Possibly, *if they had been intelligent enough to do so at that time,* something constructive might have been achieved. Instead, the movement became more and more inclined towards subversive activities and violent demands, with the result that, before long, the then president, Mr. Harry Thuku, was arrested as a political detainee. This was in the very early days of that movement."

:

"It must be stated clearly that only a *very small proportion* [italics Leakey's] of Kikuyu land relative to the whole was alienated to white settlers ...... [But by the time of WWI] quite a few Kikuyu had received a fair measure of education in our English sense, one or two had been to England and returned, and thousands had been away from their homes helping to fight the common enemy in what had been German East Africa, as members of the Carrier Corps. There was therefore a nucleus of men---mostly fairly young men---who had begun to see further than the narrow confines of their home lands, who had begun to think---*not always clearly and logically*---about the problems of their people, and so in 1922 there was born the first Kikuyu political organization, The Kikuyu Central Association, led by a band of young men fired with immense patriotism *and armed with a little learning,* who made the first slogan of their party 'We must be given back the lands which the white man has stolen from us.' "

:

"I believe however that the breakdown of the marriage custom [the payment of 'marriage insurance' in the form of livestock as a way of stabilizing marriages] is a real contributory factor in the *mental unrest and discontent* which is, in fact, responsible for the growth of the Mau Mau movement."

:

"The old training [education by elders and senior women on tribal customs and the initiation rites of the tribe] would anyhow not serve to prepare youth for the responsibilities of life as it is today, but it would certainly have been better than nothing. If no substitute could be devised, it would at least have continued to teach respect for constituted authority and the need to serve the community at the expense of individual wishes. It would also have taught the advantages of good manners, honesty and sobriety. *It can thus be said that the failure to find an adequate substitute for the character-training and preparation for citizenship,* which the age-old Kikuyu initiation rites used to give, is just one more underlying cause of the present sad state of affairs in the Kikuyu tribe."

:

It is, I think, of the utmost significance today that the leaders and also the followers of such movements as the Mau Mau are not drawn from those who are truly Christian, nor yet from those who have remained true to the old Kikuyu religion and who are horrified by the methods of Mau Mau and its teaching. *They are drawn rather from the thousands of so-called Christians, nominally, but only nominally, adherents of one or other of the Christian missions, or from the many thousands of others who belong to the separatist Kikuyu churches ....* . The Christian pastors, church elders, and genuine adherents of the various Christian missions have been unanimous in their resistance to Mau Mau and are suffering persecution and even death rather than have anything to do with it, as are the out and out followers of the old Kikuyu and so-called 'pagan' religion."

:

"Among ourselves, a large part of the character and moral training of our children is considered to be among the normal duties of the parents---and long may it remain so. There are, too, many Kikuyu parents, especially among the genuine Christians and among those who still retain faith in their ancient beliefs who try to train their children to become fit members of the adult community. But there are countless other Kikuyu children today for whom 'education' means only book learning and who are growing up without any real preparation for good citizenship and the responsibilities of modern life. *On this failure of the education system that we have introduced, in place of the old tribal one, a heavy responsibility for the troubles of today must rest.*"

:

"The surprising thing about the Kikuyu is not so much how little they have gained from European civilization, in the short space of fifty years, but how much they have absorbed and learned. It is probably because the speed of progress has been so rapid that *it has made a part of the population unbalanced in their outlook* and thus paved the way for movements like the Mau Mau, in the hands of an unscrupulous few."

A PASSAGE TO KENYA

In his last concluding chapter, Leakey does touch very briefly on the economic, political, and racial policies that were the root causes of Mau Mau, but then ends his book, as only an anthropologist might, as follows:

> "To bring this book to an end, I must briefly discuss language. Many of the difficulties of the present time are greatly increased by the fact that few Europeans can speak Kikuyu idiomatically and accurately. Although an ever increasing number of Kikuyu are learning English, it is still necessary for Europeans to use Kiswahili when talking to Kikuyu. Kiswahili is not the language of the Kikuyu or the European, and it fails lamentably as a medium of real understanding between ourselves and the average Kikuyu.
>
> *Since many Europeans are very bad at learning an African language,* and since Kikuyu is a very difficult language to learn [although every Kikuyu child learns it with ease], I feel that the teaching of English must be speeded up, in order that there be a better understanding of our policy, our laws, and our teaching. Let anyone who doubts the wisdom of this idea try to imagine the chaos that would result if a German tried to convey his ideas to the average Englishman using the French language as his medium."

Much more on point is the book of D.H. Rawcliffe, a liberal British democrat akin, say, to W. McGregor Ross, which appeared in 1954, two years after Leakey's. In his memoir, my father describes Rawcliffe's *A Struggle for Kenya* as a "careful, understanding, balanced and judicious study of the problems facing Kenya during that period of disruption and agony" and *"necessary reading* [italics mine] for any student of that difficult and dangerous period in Kenya's history. Being in parts, as it inevitably had to be, critical of the Kenya government and the European settlers, the colonial government was quick to ban it." Again, we will confine ourselves to a few additional quotations from Rawcliffe's book that speak for themselves (aside from proper names, italics are mine) and they stand in marked contrast to the earlier quotations from Leakey:

> "By 1947 two sub-cults of the *Watu wa Mungu* [this means 'People of God' in Swahili and is the name of a 1920s religious cult that arose amongst the Kikuyu] had appeared. One was the political terrorist group [that later became known as] Mau Mau. The other the *Dini ya Jesu Kristo* [a name almost self-explanatory], a localized cult which was to flare into prominence. Both were symptoms of the growing hostility of all Kikuyu movements to the Europeans and of the increasing subversive influence of the KCA and the independent schools and churches."
>
> :
>
> "In Timau [located in the White Highlands in northern part of the country at the foot of Mount Kenya], on the night of 25 September 1952, Mau Mau struck, with vindictive and brutal savagery: *two hundred and fifty sheep and cattle on European farms were butchered* or so hideously maimed that they had to be put to death. The weapon used was the *panga*, the heavy chopping-knife used by all Kikuyu. No other deed could have so hurt and enraged Kenya's settler population. It was an open and direct challenge, and many a suspected Kikuyu terrorist was shot on the least pretext as a result of the Timau slaughter before the blaze of fury it had engendered died down."
>
> :
>
> " ...by the end of September 1952 thirty-seven Africans were known to have been murdered by Mau Mau *and this was only a fraction of the true total.* Soon the terrorists were to strike at Europeans. On 3 October Mrs. [Margaret] Wright was stabbed to death on her verandah [she lived on a farm about 10 miles from Nairobi and was

the very first European victim]. ……. Four days later, Senior Chief Waruhiu, an educated man of strong personality, a Christian and a pillar of law and order, was shot dead in his car. The loyal chiefs constituted a real menace to Mau Mau, since they were the only Africans who could rally the Kikuyu against it. Three weeks later another influential chief, Senior Chief Nderi of Nyeri, was slashed to death by *pangas*. Next it was the turn of stalwart Chief Hinga. …… . Waruhiu's death roused the Government out of its torpor. Its effect upon the Kikuyu masses was electrifying. Waruhiu was an important government servant with a high degree of responsibility. By killing him Mau Mau had openly challenged the Government itself and shown the Kikuyu that it was powerless to protect its servants. … *On 20 October [1952] the Government declared a state of emergency ……"*

:

"It was also the clear intention of Mau Mau to strike a blow at the settlers by withdrawing their labour, the bulk of which was Kikuyu. A good many settlers found themselves with virtually all their labour gone; *it was even reported that one hardy settler's wife had gone out to pick pyrethrum herself.*"

:

"Ultimately a total of 100,000 men, women and children were to return to the overcrowded Kikuyu reserve. The settlers most affected averted ruin by inducing other tribes to replace their lost labour; within twelve months agricultural wages had risen by a third."

:

"It was estimated that over 90 per cent of the Kikuyu tribe had now *voluntarily or compulsorily* taken the oath of allegiance to Mau Mau. Even Government House [the Governor's residence] itself was not exempt; early in April [1953] six Kikuyu members of the staff were arrested for suspected complicity."

:

"Whether Kenyatta had actually organized Mau Mau, as the prosecution charged, may still be in dispute. What is beyond dispute, however, is that he was prepared to use Mau Mau as a lever to force the Government to grant the KAU political concessions. To attain this objective by indirectly encouraging the growth of an extremist terrorist movement under the cloak of blank innocence may not come strictly under the legal definition of 'subversive', but from the standpoint of common sense the subversive intent was clear. Kenyatta's role in the rise of Mau Mau may well have been confined to a subtle propaganda campaign operating within the actual letter of constitutional law---indeed there was little evidence to prove otherwise; but whether the deliberate fostering of a subversive movement by unscrupulous but still legal manoeuvres constituted a criminal offence was something only a judge could decide---subject to any appeal."

:

"By 22 October [1954], the [second] anniversary of the declaration of the state of emergency the security forces had killed 2,200 terrorists and camp followers, the majority of them unarmed; 700 were reported to have been wounded; more than 55,000 suspects had been tried in the courts. For its part, Mau Mau, by stealth and in combat, had killed *twenty-one Europeans and eleven Asians*; the total known African deaths amounted to 704: 451 of all races had been wounded. The cost of the emergency had now passed the Pounds 2,000,000 mark."

We will not dwell in our book on the details of Mau Mau brutality and the much greater, almost unmatched brutality of the British response. Just as the German people looked the other way from the concentration camps of Nazi Germany, the people of Kenya who were not directly affected by the colonial government's emergency measures looked the other way during the time of Mau Mau.

Rawcliffe's chapter titled "Terror and Counter-Terror" in his aforementioned book is essential reading in its entirety and he is fairly accurate on the cited European and Asian casualties. But even he greatly underestimates the extent of government-sponsored terror and the resulting African, primarily Kikuyu, suffering, which has only been fully revealed to the British public very recently. A more accurate accounting is given in *Secret History*, a series that aired on Channel Four Television in Britain in 1999, with a written account provided by Barbara Slaughter titled "How Britain crushed the 'Mau Mau rebellion'." She reports that

> "...the LFA [Land Freedom Army, the now-preferred synonym for Mau Mau] death toll during the emergency was 11,500, of whom about 1,000 were hanged. Eighty thousand Kikuyu were imprisoned in concentration camps. One hundred and fifty thousand Africans, mostly Kikuyu, lost their lives, many dying of disease and starvation in the "protected villages" [into which non-detainees were herded on the Kikuyu Reservation in order better to control them]. On the other side, the LFA killed around 2,000 people [mostly Africans], including 32 European civilians and 63 members of the security forces [the dozen or so Asians are not mentioned explicitly]."

As for the general policy of the Government, Piers Brendon's chapter titled *"Uhuru* – Freedom: Kenya and the Mau Mau" within his monumental 2007 work, *The Decline and Fall of the British Empire: 1781-1997*, to which we have already made extensive reference in Chapter 2, is also necessary reading for any student of the entire, heart-wrenching story. Specifically he says the following with reference to government policy during the emergency: "In the opinion of a recent critic, he [Sir Evelyn Baring, the then-Governor of Kenya] was laying the foundations of one of the most brutal and 'restrictive police states in the history of the empire' " and that "throughout their imperial history the British always paid lip service to legality, but by the mid-1950s it was an open secret that Kenya had become a police state that dispensed racist terror. After all Dr. Malan, the Nationalist Prime Minister of South Africa, took it as a model for his apartheid regime." Finally, for a description of the horrors endured by a particular Kikuyu detainee, see J.M. Kariuki's *'Mau Mau' Detainee.*

Let us put everything in perspective: *about as many Europeans and Asians civilians were killed as were taken by lions during the building of the railway at the turn of the century,* thereby creating a similar level of terror! Two hundred and fifty cattle and sheep belonging to European settlers were slaughtered at the outset of the rebellion! One settler's wife was actually forced to pick her own pyrethrum! Meanwhile, well over a *hundred thousand* African civilians lost their lives---a number reminiscent of the number of natives who died in East Africa as a consequence of WWI---and many more were disrupted or displaced.

By the end of 1955, Mau Mau was crushed militarily. It began as an outpouring of Kikuyu rage against the colonial government and evolved into a civil war within the Kikuyu tribe itself, and, fortunately for the British, Mau Mau went off half-cocked and did not spread widely to other tribes. The movement did not achieve either of its long-term objectives, namely, independence and land restoration, although it hastened their attainment. In its shorter term objectives it was more successful, by denying the white settlers their endless supply of cheap labor, and by dismantling the "loyalist" infrastructure put in place by the colonial government to dominate the native tribes. But this was achieved at the cost of great suffering to the Kikuyu people.

The state of emergency itself did not formally end until 1959 when many detainees began to be released. In J.M. Kariuki's case, release did not come until 1960. He and the other Kikuyu activists and freedom fighters of his generation adored Kenyatta and, a year later, Kariuki and several newly-freed companions visited Kenyatta in detention, only a few months before the latter's own release. In his aforementioned memoir, Kariuki describes his feelings during this audience with his revered leader:

> "There, framed in the doorway, waiting for us, was *Mzee* [revered old man in Swahili]. He greeted us in a wonderful manner and as he embraced me to him I felt like a tiny chicken being folded under its mother's wings; all my worries and troubles now belonged to him. This would be a small burden indeed for a man who had already taken the suffering of all our people on himself. .... No African who loves his country can ever forget the man who has shown us the way to freedom and who has undergone so much for us. There are a few Africans who hold other things dearer than their love of country: God, peace, wealth, drink or women. These few might genuinely say that they do not like *Mzee*; others might say it through fear. But the living, throbbing, bustling, laughing, crying, bursting mass of our people love him more than anything else they know. He is our chosen leader and he alone will lead us out of the past, out of the deep pits of dark memories to the bright future of our country. Kenyatta does not depend on K.A.D.U. or K.A.N.U. [the two recently formed political parties, but sadly already exhibiting the tribal fracturing of the country], Indian Congress or Indian Freedom Party, New Kenya Party or Coalition, he is more than any political party. He does not speak of his people as detainees, loyalists, terrorists, Home Guards, 'Mau Mau', Catholics, Protestants, Muslims, Asians, Europeans. Kenyatta is greater than any Kikuyu, he is greater than any Luo or Nandi or Masai or Giriama, he is greater than any Kenyan, he is the greatest African of them all. He knows not tribe, nor race, he bears no hatred or malice for the past; he is human and yet wiser than any other

human being I have ever known. They are all his people, his responsibility and his children: all fellow human beings to love and to cherish, to correct if they do wrong, to praise if they do right."

Two years later, in December, 1963, the very year when the above adoring words of Kariuki appeared in print, Jomo Kenyatta became the first President of an independent Kenya and he remained so until his death in 1978. Under his presidency the Kikuyu tribe took over the dominant role previously occupied by the white settlers. But sadly, things did not go well for idealists like Kariuki, an avowed socialist, or even for other surviving Mau Mau freedom fighters. In 1975, he vanished without trace after last being seen with Kenyatta's bodyguards. Other prominent politicians, who like J.M. Kariuki were initially ardent supporters but later grew to oppose Kenyatta's post-independence policies, were likewise assassinated.

As for Harry Thuku, the other great leader of the independence movement in Kenya, he died peacefully in 1970, a well-established landowner and farmer, a few months before the publication of his autobiography. During the emergency, he had been viewed by the Kikuyu as siding with the loyalist chiefs, many of whom had been killed by the Mau Mau, and he explains his survival as follows (italics mine):

"But the most interesting thing about my own safety I heard after the emergency from George Ndegwa [another detainee whose long involvement dated back to serving as acting general secretary of the banned KCA]. He had just been released, so I offered him a lift to Nairobi, and we had a discussion in a milk-bar. He told me that Kenyatta had issued an order from detention that I was not to be killed by the Mau Mau; this letter was even taken to the forest fighters. *He said I was to be left safe, for I had been the bridge they had crossed to get to where they were today.*"

Today, tomorrow, perhaps forever! Wheels, within wheels, within wheels! And, as if to place yet another exclamation mark at the end of the Mau Mau tragedy, the British Government issued a formal apology in 2013 for having condoned torture during the emergency, and along with this apology came an offer of compensation to surviving Mau Mau detainees, thus bringing to a formal conclusion this most recent cycle in the age-old history of empire.

The Four Leaders (clockwise): Delamere, Grogan, Kenyatta, Thuku

Chapter 12

J.M. NAZARETH, Q.C., M.L.C.

At the time of the volcano-like eruption of violence called Mau Mau, my father and his family were away in Bombay. In a decision reminiscent of my paternal grandfather having sent his wife and children to India just before the outbreak of World War I, my father had chosen to take an extended holiday in India, following his dramatic resignation, in April, 1952, from the office of President of the Kenya Indian Congress (as described in a previous chapter). He was temporarily free of political responsibilities and his legal practice could be scheduled in a flexible way, and thus, in August 1952, our entire family left for India. What his motivation was for taking this decision, whether it was by design or by default, I do not know. It is hard to believe that, in mid-1952, my father was completely unaware of the gathering storm. Perhaps it was some premonition of disaster, or perhaps it was a meeting with Prime Minister Nehru arranged for later that year. I never had reason to ask him, as I now wish I had.

Exactly two years earlier, in August 1950, my father had delivered the emotion-laden address as newly-elected President of the KIC at a session held in the town of Eldoret---the very heart of the White Highlands. In his own words, taken from his memoir (italics mine):

> "What my Presidential address did was to give vigorous expression to the sentiment against racial discrimination felt no less keenly by Africans than by Indians, and thus I in effect acted as spokesman of Indians and Africans alike, giving expression to feelings deeply felt by both communities. *I had not at the time I delivered the address the slightest inkling of the existence of Mau Mau* [in mid-1950] or that a nationalist movement had been quietly building up among the Africans. That it was is clear, since Mau Mau was declared "to be a society dangerous to the good movement" of the Colony by an order of the Governor in council dated August 12, 1950, a few days after my address [as noted by Rawcliffe in the previous chapter, at that time Mau Mau was viewed as a *dangerous sub-cult* of a quasi-religious Kikuyu cult known as *Watu wa Mungu*, and not a separate organization]. As an expression, therefore, of strong feeling prevalent among the Africans and Indians the address had an importance and relevance well beyond myself. As an expression of contemporary attitudes and feelings of Indians and Africans it has a value which it would otherwise not have had. As a genuine expression of what has always lain and still lies at the roots of my own thinking it is of the highest personal significance to me."

What better evidence is there of the strong confluence between the anti-discrimination aspirations of the African natives and the Indian immigrants, on the one hand, and of the two communities seeming to occupy two completely different universes, on the other. The political institutions, within which their social and political objectives were expressed, namely, the Kenya Indian Congress (KIC) and the Kenya African Union (KAU), proceeded on paths that ran parallel to one another, and joint sessions between them, or even meetings between their respective executive committees, were organized only at rare intervals. Within the KIC, the sectarian divide between Muslims and Hindus, which had separated Pakistan from India, was the central fissure. Within the KAU, the fracture was between the "loyalist" Kikuyu, who sought tribal advancement in co-operation with the colonial authority, and other members of the tribe, who simply wanted to be rid of this white settler-dominated authority altogether and achieve rapid and complete independence from Britain. (It was within the latter group that the highly secretive Mau Mau society had slowly gathered strength after World War II.) The governor of the colony and his settler allies were able to exploit the intra-community fissures, which were amplified by a natural animosity between Indians and Africans arising from economic disparity and mutual color prejudice, to further their policy of "divide and rule."

Following its proscription by the government, Mau Mau continued to secretly organize during the period 1950-1952, and it was in September, 1952, during the time of our family's extended visit to India, that the rebellion had erupted prematurely into the open. Jomo Kenyatta was arrested soon afterwards and his trial date was set in November of that year. My father did not return to Kenya until December, and, as he recounts in his memoir: "Had I been in Kenya at the time of his arrest I think it is not unlikely that he would have asked me to appear for him as one of his [legal] counsel, and I would not have refused. But any such situation did not arise owing to my absence in India at that time of crisis." Much earlier, for much of the period 1930-1934, my father and Jomo Kenyatta had both been residents in London. At that time, my father was entirely focused on his legal education, and Kenyatta, a man almost twice my father's age at the time, was coming into his own in a quite different way, and there appears to have been no contact between them. This curious *non*-intersection between their life paths during their formative years and now again at the start of the Mau Mau emergency was indeed symptomatic of the lack of intersection, despite close physical proximity, between the political and social lives of the Indian immigrants and the native Africans of Kenya.

Mau Mau created a wedge, for the first time, between the political struggles of the Indians and the Africans. The emergency was declared, by coincidence, at the time of the next KIC congress, which was held in late 1952, and the Indians, like the "loyalist" Africans, were forced to take sides. As Rawcliffe notes, the vast majority of Kenya Indians were solidly anti-Mau Mau, which had "very definitely scared them." My father too was a firm believer in legal process, the very bedrock of his existence, and he describes the years between 1952 and 1955 as "a period during which Mau Mau was active and I was becalmed." Removed from political activity, he redirected his energies instead towards his legal practice. It was during this time that he became the first non-European to be appointed to the judiciary, a temporary assignment which he describes in his memoir as being (italics mine):

> "...an acting judgeship in 1953, expected to last about three weeks to try Mau Mau cases carrying a mandatory death sentence. Offers had been made to ... [two other Indian lawyers]... both of whom had served as presidents of the Kenya Law Society. It was not until 1954, in the year after the judgeship, that I was elected president [of the Law Society]. *I was the third Indian offered the appointment.* My wife was against my accepting, fearing the danger believed to be involved. Asians had been complaining for many years about not being appointed to the Judiciary. *For that reason and because I considered it the duty of citizens to assist in the maintenance of law and order I felt bound to accept this unwelcome offer.* However, I thought I should consult

Apa Pant, the Indian High Commissioner. As he was of the same opinion, I had any doubts removed, and I accepted. In the event, the tenure lasted about five weeks instead of the expected three. When, however, the registrar suggested that I continue or serve for another period I declined. The obligations of my [legal] practice demanded my return and I had found the strain of trying a bullet case (being found with a bullet in your possession) which also carried a mandatory death sentence, unbearable. [This also gives a further illustration of the draconian nature of the emergency laws put in place by the colonial administration, which has been already mentioned in a previous chapter.] In that case I had been able to acquit the accused, for it was not until the third search after he had been in police custody for an hour or some hours or possibly days, that the bullet was claimed to have been found in his shirt. But I felt myself unable to face another trial of a bullet case. ....

[Years later, a well-known Indian who had actively sided with the Kikuyu during the emergency and been detained by the administration], in about 1971, at a party criticized to me my acceptance of the appointment, but, when I explained to him my reasons, *he said I should have explained them to the Africans as they held it against me.* If they did, I can see no justification whatever for their having done so."

This well illustrates my father's legalistic approach, wherein adherence to principle took precedence over the building of alliances---hardly a prescription for success in the political sphere. It was during those difficult years of Mau Mau that my father's career in law began to blossom, entering its golden age. Soon he would be elected vice-president and then president of the Kenya Law Society and elevated to the rank of Queen's Counsel (Q.C) within the legal profession. He was also temporarily active, for the first time, in the political life of the local Goan community, siding with the faction that sought freedom for Goa from Portuguese colonial rule and a reintegration with independent India. It was also during this period that Rawcliffe had visited Kenya and had written his definitive book on Mau Mau, and we can draw upon his first-hand, acute observations after interviewing my father (again italics mine):

> "One of the most active Asian politicians before the emergency was J.M. Nazareth, now vice-president of the Law Society of Kenya and an ex-president of the K.I.C. [Kenya Indian Congress], of which he now holds merely an *ex-officio* position. Nazareth is an intelligent and able Goan lawyer. Since the emergency he has been appointed a puisne judge---the first Asian to attain such a position. *He struck me as being the one Asian in Kenya capable of becoming an outstanding political leader.* It is his aim to bring Africans and Asians together in their natural struggle against the racial discrimination of the Europeans and he holds that the only answer to the British policy of perpetuating the tribalization of Kenya is African nationalism, a view fully shared by the moderates of the now banned K.A.U. [Kenya African Union]. He believes there is no future for Kenya unless the existing racial divisions are broken down; the divisions, he has said, should be inter-racial and based solely on political and economic lines.
>
> Nazareth advocates allowing Africans and Asians into the good residential areas round Nairobi provided the exteriors of the houses are kept up to standard. He would also like to see a number of Asians farming in the white highlands but realizes that this might result in arousing the hostility of the Africans. He urges the opening up of the white highlands to Africans either on a cooperative basis or under government supervision so that the land will be properly farmed.
>
> *There can be no doubt about Nazareth's strong sympathies for the African nationalists;* it was he who helped to draw up the twenty-four 'demands' of the K.A.U. a few months before that organization was

proscribed. It was he who took on the unwanted job of leading the team of seven defence counsel defending the seventy-three Kikuyu charged with murder in the Lari massacre. It is unlikely that he approves the present policy of the K.I.C. and he would agree with those who have criticized it for failing to support Delhi's official policy of aiding the Kikuyu to free themselves 'from the injustices imposed upon them by the Kenya Government'. Nazareth is no extremist judged by the contemporary standards in Kenya politics; but he sees the need for drastic changes and his ability will undoubtedly give him a leading role to play in the colony's future.

The official leaders of the various Asian groups have none of Nazareth's political acumen and lack the qualities necessary for mass leadership. They are sound, sensible men, conservative and well-to-do. While they share their followers' social and political aspirations and realize the need to co-operate with the Africans, their approach is purely constitutional and many Asians regard them as mere 'stooges' of the British."

And thus it is easy to see why political fortune once again came knocking at my father's door. One evening, early in 1956, he was in the dressing room getting attired for a formal dinner of the Kenya Law Society when he received an unexpected visit from two or three young Indian activists from Nakuru, a town located in the Rift Valley about a hundred miles from Nairobi. What had they come for? Nothing less than to ask him to stand as a candidate for the Legislative Council of Kenya (popularly known as Legco) for the Western Electoral Region. In his memoir, he describes the considerations that led him to accept this invitation that came "out of the blue" and the ensuing hard-fought campaign against two seasoned and well-established candidates who had previously held that office, which resulted in his election to the seat by a narrow margin. The 1956-1960 period of his membership in Legco is covered in great detail in my father's memoir---a major strength of the book--- and it would do him a disservice to attempt to summarize it here, save to say that he played a major role in Kenya's political transformation during this period. These turbulent four years culminated in the Round Table Conference held at Lancaster House in London in early 1960, when Britain agreed for the first time to Kenyan independence, and the dominant European community lost power to the African majority. It was also during this time that my father refined the arguments he had marshaled against artificial religion-based electorates, during his earlier presidency of the KIC, into a political "philosophy" wherein he argued equally strongly against *a pure form of common electoral roll based on a universal franchise*. As he expressed it himself (italics mine): "in the interests of Africans and non-Africans alike [I] consistently advocated a *tailored form of common roll* which would help to foster good will and co-operation between the various communities in Kenya and would help to promote the election of Africans who, while fully representative of their community, would yet be moderate in their outlook and understanding in their policies, politicians who would maintain the good will and mutual understanding between Africans and non-Africans so essential to the progress and prosperity of Kenya, a form of common roll which would keep out race-haters and race-baiters, the rabid and the racial." *Ever the principled maverick in the political sphere,* this endeared him to neither the Europeans, who were losing power, nor the Africans, who had newly gained it, and not even to other leaders of the Indian community, who were busy currying favor with the new African leadership. Full detail on this pivotal period can be found in my father's memoir *Brown Man Black Country*, but there is one item that one will not find in it that is worth quoting in full, namely, the following letter penned by him towards the end of his tenure and dated 23rd August 1960, which was later republished under the heading "Act of Wisdom & Grace had

Better Come Now" in the 1963 collection *Struggle for Release Jomo and his Colleagues*, a compilation by A.H. Patel:

> "Long before the ending of the Emergency I have advocated the release of all who had served their sentences or who were detained without trial, unless it was clearly shown that they were to be a danger to security. It was my view that on the completion of the term of his sentence Mr. Jomo Kenyatta should have been released, though a few months ago I became somewhat shaken in this view when I was told by certain distinguished visitors, who had been afforded facilities to go round the country and who had excellent opportunities to check on public opinion, that the effect of his release on a large section of the Kikuyu tribe, particularly the loyalists, would be unfortunate, and that they were opposed to his release and were afraid of its consequences.
>
> Having discussed this point with a distinguished Kikuyu of great political experience I think the views of these visitors are mistaken. I think it is right and desirable that Kenyatta should be released. I do not think that he constitutes a present threat to security and there is therefore no sufficient justification for denying him his liberty. I feel that any advantages gained by restricting him are greatly outweighed by the disadvantages and by the unfortunate effect on Non-European opinion.
>
> With the clear declaration of the goal of British policy made at Lancaster House there is, I think, no likelihood of his supporting any unconstitutional struggle. On the other hand he may well end or greatly reduce the tendency of some African leaders to try to gain support among Africans by attacks on the minority races or by outbidding one another in irresponsible appeals to extremism or racialism. Possessing an unchallenged ascendancy over other African leaders, which frees him from the temptation or need to advocate such

damaging policies to win or maintain public support, he can, if he desires, be an effective, moderating influence, which could greatly help to restore or maintain political and economic stability and confidence in the country.

Delay in releasing him does not improve, it can only worsen the situation. With the General Elections early next year, the Government would be immediately faced with a resolution of the Legislative Council demanding his immediate release. The act of wisdom and grace had better come now.

J.M. NAZARETH, M.L.C."

So typical of my father, the letter itself being written with wisdom and grace and from a position of principle!

My father's political life ended with the legislative session of December, 1960. By then he had moved his family from the little rented house on Forest Road to a magnificent, five-bedroom, multi-balconied, stone mansion, designed for him and my mother by a well-known Nairobi architect-cum-builder (of Italian origin), and located in an upscale district of the city. He struggled manfully on, continuing in his very successful legal practice, writing his memoir, even seeking solace in the works of the renowned Indian political activist turned spiritual leader, Vivekenanda, but he did not find any further political role to play in independent Kenya. The meeting long ago with Prime Minister Nehru, marking the end of the first major cycle of his political life, when he had entreated with Nehru to cease referring to the Kenya Indians as "guests" of the African, continued to reverberate in his mind, and thus it is fitting to end this historical collage by quoting the emotion-laden poem, titled "To the African: 'No Guest am I'," with which my father opened his memoir (italics mine):

A PASSAGE TO KENYA

"Why do you call me 'guest',
When here I have my home,
When here my father lived and died,
My mother too, and a brother?
Their graves lie there within this City's bounds,
Where I myself was born,
My children too---all three of them.

Must they and I leave this land,
Be strangers to it
Because your skin is black and mine and theirs is brown,
Your folk came here some scores of years ere ours?

Why do you not hold out your hands
In friendship, and call me friend,
In love and call me brother,
And bid me stay and help to build this land,
Give me warm assurance, dispel my fears.
By deed, not by words alone?
If love and friendship be not in you,
Let justice rule your thoughts:
Shame not the past nor the years to come.

That I am guest I do deny.
But when you'd drive me out how can I stay?
I lack the power, and now may be I lack the will.
The day is late for change of mind.
Yet even now I'd change, for fain I'd stay,
If justice blest this land,

Or warm hearts bid me stay
And warm hands held me close
And told me 'tarry',
'Tarry to the end of your days.
This land is yours as it is mine,
This is your home as it is mine;
No guest of mine art thou, but friend and brother,
This home, this land, of ours, our joined hands must make it great'."

This home, this land of interchanging savannah and forest, which 200,000 years ago had seen the birth of modern Homo Sapiens, and which, over the course of millennia, had become populated by a quilted patchwork of African tribes, whose racial types, customs, and cultures were as diverse as the many species of animals that roamed the high plains of Eastern Africa. Then, over the brief passage of just the first six decades of the 20th century, the knowledge and capital brought to East Africa by British and other European immigrants as heirs to the industrial revolution, the unique ability of Indian immigrants to advance commerce on a shoestring, and the exploited, backbreaking labor of the native African, all had melded together to create the modern, independent nation of Kenya.

My father, John Maximian Nazareth Q.C., M.L.C., continued to reside in independent Kenya's capital city of Nairobi for another quarter century, increasingly saddened by the post-independence conflict that pitted tribe against tribe and African against Indian, still viewed, until his death in 1989, as a "guest." At his request, he was laid to rest within his father's grave, in the cemetery at the foot of Forest Road, now forgotten and grown wild.

BIBLIOGRAPHY

Aiyar, Sana (2015), *Indians in Kenya: The Politics of Diaspora*, Harvard University Press, Cambridge, Massachusetts, USA.

Barnes, Juliet (2013), *The Ghosts of Happy Valley: Searching for the Lost World of Africa's Infamous Aristocrats*, Aurum Press, London, UK.

Bennett, George (1963), *Kenya - A Political History: The Colonial Period*, Oxford University Press, London, UK.

Boyes, John (1911), *King of the Wa-Kikuyu*, Methuen, London, UK. Republished in Resnick's Library of African Adventure, Alexander Books, North Carolina, USA, 2001.

Brendon, Piers (2007), *The Decline and Fall of the British Empire 1781-1997*, Vintage Books, Random House, New York, USA.

Brittain, H. and Ripley, P.J.G. (1963), *A Simple History of East Africa*, Collins, London and Glasgow, UK.

Brockway, Fenner (1955), *African Journeys*, Victor Gollancz, London, UK.

Carita, Helder (1997), *Palaces of Goa: Models and Types of Indo-Portuguese Civil Architecture*, Cartago, London, UK.

Carvalho, Selma (2014), *A Railway Runs Through*, CinnamonTeal Publishing, Goa, India.

Cottineau de Kloguen, Denis Louis (1831), *An Historical Sketch of Goa, The Metropolis of the Portuguese Settlements in India*, The Madras Literary Society, Madras, India. Republished under the title: *Cottineau's History of Goa,* B.X. Furtado & Sons, Bombay, India, 1922.

Cransworth, Lord (1939), *Kenya Chronicles*, Macmillan, London, UK.

Delf, George (1963), *Asians in East Africa*, Oxford University Press, London, UK.

De Souza, Teotonio R. (1986), *Some Historical Notes on Moira*, in *Moira: A Peep into its Past*, 350 Years Thanksgiving Celebration of the Church of Moira, 1636-1986, Goa, India.

Dinesen, Isak (1937), *Out of Africa*, Vintage Books, Random House, New York, USA.

Farson, Negley (1940), *Behind God's Back*, Victor Gollancz, London, UK.

French, Patrick (2012), *India: A Portrait*, Vintage Books, Random House, New York, USA.

Grogan, E.S. & Sharp, A.H. (1900), *From the Cape to Cairo: The First Traverse of Africa from South to North*, Hurst & Blackett, London, UK.

Gunther, John (1955), *Inside Africa*, Hamish Hamilton, London, UK.

Hobley, Charles (1970), *Kenya: From Chartered Company to Crown Colony*, Second Edition, Frank Cass & Company, London, UK. (First Edition, 1929).

Huxley, Elspeth and Perham, Margery (1944), *Race and Politics in Kenya*, Faber and Faber, London, UK (with an introduction by Lord Lugard).

James, William (1901), *The Varieties of Religious Experience: A Study in Human Nature*, A Mentor Book, The New American Library, New Jersey, USA. (The Gifford Lectures on Natural Religion delivered at Edinburgh in 1901-1902.)

Judt, Tony (2010), *Ill Fares the Land*, Penguin Books, New York, USA.

Kariuki, J.M. (1963), *'Mau Mau' Detainee*, Oxford University Press, London, UK.

Kenyatta, Jomo (1938), *Facing Mount Kenya*, Secker & Warburg, London, UK (with an Introduction by B. Malinowski).

Leakey, L.S.B. (1952), *Mau Mau and the Kikuyu*, Methuen & Company, London, UK.

Linschoten, Jan Huyghen van (1610), *Histoire de la Navigation et de son Voyage es Indes Orientales*, Amsterdam, The Netherlands.

Mangat, J.S. (1969), *The History of Asians in East Africa c. 1886 to 1945*, Oxford Studies in African Affairs, Oxford University Press, London, UK.

Markham, Beryl (1943), *West with the Night*, reprinted by North Point Press, Berkeley and San Francisco, USA, 1983.

Mascarenhas-Keyes, Stella (2011), *Colonialism, Migration & The International Catholic Goan Community*, Goa 1556, Saligao, Goa, India.

Mendonsa, Gilda (1997), *The Best of Goan Cooking*, Hippocrene Books, New York, USA.

Murray-Brown, Jeremy (1972), *Kenyatta*, George Allen & Unwin, London, UK.

Nazareth, J.L. (1996), *Reminiscences of an Ex-Brahmin: Portraits of a Journey through India*, Apollo Printing, Berkeley, California, USA.

Nazareth, J.M. (1981), *Brown Man Black Country: On the Foothills of Uhuru*, Tidings Publications, New Delhi, India. (Also available as an E-book published by Goa 1556, Saligao, Goa, India, August, 2015).

Nehru, Jawaharlal (1946), *The Discovery of India*, Oxford University Press, London, UK.

Obama, Barack (1995), *Dreams from my Father: A Story of Race and Inheritance*, Three Rivers Press, Random House, New York, USA.

Pandit, Heta (2004), *In and Around Old Goa*, Marg Publications, Mumbai, India.

Patel, A.H. (1963), *Struggle for Release Jomo and his Colleagues*, New Kenya Publishers, Nairobi, Kenya.

Patterson, J.H. (1907), *The Man-Eaters of Tsavo*, Macmillan, London, UK.

Pringle, Patrick (1954), *The Story of a Railway*, Evans Brothers Limited, Russell Square, London, UK.

Pyrard de Laval, Francois (1615), *Travels to the East Indies*, Vol. II, Paris, France.

Rawcliffe, D.H. (1954), *The Struggle for Kenya*, Victor Gollancz, London, UK.

Speke, John Hanning (1863), *Journal of the Discovery of the Source of the Nile*, W. Blackwood & Sons, Edinburgh, UK.

The Goa League (1956), *Goa: The Goan Point of View*, Independent Publishing Company, London, UK.

Thuku, Harry (1970), *An Autobiography*, Oxford University Press (Eastern Africa), Nairobi, Kenya (with assistance from Kenneth King).

Trzebinski, Errol (1985), *The Kenya Pioneers*, W.W. Norton & Company, New York, USA and London, UK.

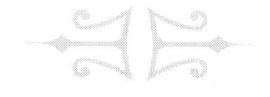

AUTHOR'S BIOGRAPHY

John Lawrence (Larry) Nazareth was born in 1946 in Nairobi, Kenya, of Indian (Goan) parentage and attended high schools in Nairobi and Bombay---today's Mumbai. He graduated from Cambridge University (Trinity College), England, with a B.A. in Mathematics and a Diploma in Computer Science. He then immigrated to the United States to continue his education at the University of California, Berkeley, where he obtained a Ph.D. in Computer Science and, simultaneously, an M.Sc. in Industrial Engineering and Operations Research.

His professional life, which began in 1973, has spanned scientific research, consulting, and university teaching. He has held appointments on the research staff at Argonne National Laboratory (University of Chicago), the Systems Optimization Laboratory (Stanford University), and the International Institute for Applied Systems Analysis (Vienna, Austria); he was also engaged on a variety of consulting projects by the San Francisco firm, Woodward-Clyde Consultants (subsequently merged with URS Corporation). His academic career began in 1988-89 when he was tenured as a full Professor in the Department of Pure and Applied Mathematics at Washington State University (Pullman, WA) and, soon thereafter, appointed Affiliate Professor in the Department of Applied Mathematics at the University of Washington (Seattle, WA). He retired from academic teaching in 2003 and now makes his home on Bainbridge Island near Seattle, Washington.

He has written seven books in the mathematical and algorithmic sciences under the imprint of Oxford University Press, Springer-Verlag, and other scientific presses, and he has published extensively in the research journals of that field. In pursuing broader interests, he has also written essays on algorithms and analytics, which have appeared in technical magazines and newsletters such as *OR/MS Today, SIAM News, Journal of the Cambridge Computer Lab Ring*, and *SIAG/OPT Views-and-News*, where he served as its founding editor from 1992-96; and he has independently published a booklet of poetry, *Three Faces of God and Other Poems* (1986), a travelogue, *Reminiscences of an Ex-Brahmin: Portraits of a Journey through India* (1996), and a three-act play, *The Tease Spoons* (2016).

For further background information, please visit www.math.wsu.edu/faculty/nazareth

Made in the USA
Charleston, SC
10 February 2017